To Christine,

Best wishes,

Alan Howe

'Training never stops'

18th April 2017.

First hardback edition printed 2015 in the United Kingdom.

A catalogue record for this book is available from the British Library.

ISBN 978-0-9935029-0-3

Published by Adrian Howe.
For more copies of this book, please email:
mail@dog-whisperer.me.uk
Tel: 01455 828748

Designed and set by Alliance Creative
www.alliancecreative.co.uk

Printed in Great Britain.

Acknowledgements

Elaine Wood, Wendy Shipp, Sarah Eley and Dave Walker, Joanne Walton, Monica Newell, Evelyn Burnside and Rob Manley, Patricia and Jens Freeborn, Clare Blakemore and Gary Denham, Penny and Mike O'Callaghan, Sarah and John Catton. Special thanks to Sylvia Howe for making sense of my ramblings and Steve Johnstone for his innovative design in the production of this book.

INTROD

I've never seen a dog give a treat to another dog.

I've never seen a dog praise another dog.

Yet dogs seem to be able to communicate effectively with other dogs and get along just fine even if they are from another country.

I have worked with dogs from Ireland, France, Spain, Portugal, Romania, Tobago and Australia. They seemed to understand me and my dogs quite easily and it really got me thinking.

'Dog' seems to be an international language but most humans cannot speak it.

So why can't humans understand and communicate with dogs more effectively?

I think humans expect dogs to understand humans and our weird world. Dogs clearly don't understand most humans otherwise there would be no need for dog rescue centres.

I believe that we humans should try to understand how dogs communicate with each other and then try to simulate those signals to get the dog to do what we want.

Understanding the dog mind and how dogs interact together is the subject of many bad books and I am regularly told by my clients that they are totally confused by the conflicting information obtained from the TV, internet, books and dog professionals

This book is a practical guide to controlling your dog inside and outside the house, so that you and your dog can live contentedly together.

I do not touch on the training methods for gundogs, sheep dogs or other specialised work. I have no experience or expertise in those fields. This book is for the average pet dog owner who may be struggling to rehabilitate their dog in certain situations and needs a quick and permanent fix to their problem.

Owners can learn to use methods that really work to cure the most common behavioural problems.

This book will show you how to control your dog by using its natural instincts, without the need for treats, clickers or gadgets. The techniques described are simple, quick and effective.

Forget theories. You won't find any in these pages.

These practical methods have evolved by working with and curing hundreds of dogs.

Controlling your dog is not rocket science.

If you follow my methods, you and your dog will have a much deeper bond and understand each other better than ever before.

The book includes real case histories to illustrate how even the most difficult dog can be rehabilitated. It assesses techniques currently being used by dog trainers and behaviourists. You will see what I think of these pretty quickly! You will find it hard to believe some of the things my clients have been told and some of the training techniques thrust upon unsuspecting owners and their dogs.

To help you choose the right trainer for your dog, there is a list of questions for you to ask them, with the right and the wrong answers. If a trainer gives the wrong answer, keep your money in your pocket. Many, for instance, have recommended to clients that their 'aggressive' dog be put down. All too often the dog is more frightened than aggressive and with a little leadership and direction it turns out to be a wonderful pet.

About the Author

I am a specialist dog trainer. I train problem dogs. The dogs that have been asked to leave training classes. The barking dogs. The anti-social dogs. The aggressive dogs other trainers won't handle. I meet dogs under sentence of death for biting another dog or human.

I am often their last chance.

I don't run weekly training classes for good dogs. That doesn't interest me. Standing around a village hall with 10 or 20 owners for an hour getting their dogs to sit, stay and shake a paw while stuffing them full of treats is boring and a waste of everyone's time.

I can get a dog to sit and stay in two minutes or less without using a command or a treat but by using **a dog technique** on a dog. A technique you can learn very easily – you will find it in the Chapter entitled **The General and the Sentry** but hang on, don't rush straight to it. There are other things you need to know first. You will learn techniques which will give you an insight into a dog's mind. Simple and clear methods you can use to get the dog to do what you want quickly and easily. And your life with your dog will be transformed.

Understanding the signals

Your dog is giving out signals all the time. Visual and vocal signals. I will help you to interpret those signals so that you understand what the dog is trying to tell you.

Here's an example which may make you smile. I was sitting on the sofa with my better half one night. My Border Collie Pip was lying by the other sofa craning his neck to look at me.

'What do you think he is trying to tell us?' I asked her.

'I think he just loves you,' she answered. 'He can't take his eyes off you.'

'No that's not it,' I told her. 'He is telling me the lollipop stick I just threw his way has slipped under the sofa and he can't reach it, so he wants me to stand up and get it for him.'

I stood up and asked 'Where is it?'

He looked under the sofa and tapped his paw on the floor. I retrieved the stick and we played fetch for a couple of minutes. I had understood his signals.

Pip would retrieve a discarded matchstick if he thought there was the slightest chance of a game of fetch. For those who are worried, he was in no danger of swallowing the lollipop stick. He was too smart for that.

My methods work on every dog

Many people think that it takes two or three months to change a dog's behaviour. It doesn't. It can take **two or three hours**, whatever the size, breed or age.

The methods I use work on **every** dog. It's the owners I usually have problems training.

Need convincing? I would too, if I were you. You can read a number of genuine case histories on my website: **www.dog-whisperer.me.uk** and follow the link to an independent review site with testimonials from satisfied customers.

No dog is born vicious or genuinely tries to annoy you. It is just being a dog.

I teach people to understand their dogs, and dogs to understand their humans.

That's it, in a nutshell. And that is what makes the difference.

Contents

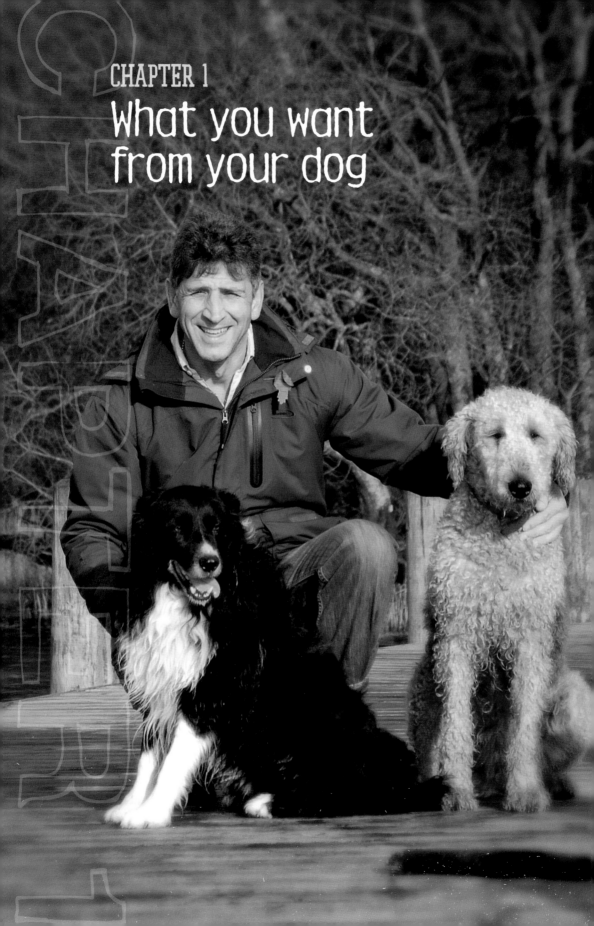

CHAPTER 1
What you want from your dog

What you want from your dog

I routinely ask owners what they want from their dog. Usually there are no more than a dozen wishes.

The average dog owner's wish list

- I want a dog that will come when called and go away when told
- I dream of walking my dog on a lead without it pulling
- I want my dog to meet and greet other dogs and people in a calm and friendly manner
- Getting my dog to sit and stay when told would be brilliant

Inside the house it would be great if…

- It didn't mess or scent mark on my carpets or furniture
- It didn't jump all over visitors and pester them to play
- It didn't eat the mail or try to remove the postman's fingers
- It could be left on its own and not fret, whine, bark, mess or destroy the house or my possessions and furniture
- It didn't mouth or bite arms, ankles, trouser bottoms or sleeves
- It allowed me to take its food, toys or other items away without growling, snarling or biting
- It would bark at the door but stop barking when commanded and relax
- It would stay calm and allow the vet to examine and treat it

Why don't you get what you want from your dog?

Your dog does not understand what you are trying to get it to do. There is a lack of communication. This can lead to frustration and sometimes anger.

Most dog training books start along these lines. 'Use positive reinforcement and equip yourself with lots of treats'. If you don't want to use a treat-based method you are pretty much on your own.

You may not want to use treat training because your dog has a small stomach or is just not that interested in food. You may not like the idea of constantly bribing your dog to do things and having to carry smelly treats every time you want to go for a walk.

I have been told numerous times that a dog has been physically sick because it had been fed so many treats and consequently the owner stopped going to the training class.

Where does that leave you?

A new approach

This book will help you to achieve your wish list and understand your dog.

The methods used are simple and quick and the logic is undeniable.

Pip's Story

Pip 30/01/2002 – 09/11/2013

Pip was a full male border collie. I thought I would make that clear as people would often think Pip was short for Pippa and were surprised to find he was a male because of his gentle nature. He came to me from Sandra and Bob Cook of Lancashire in the August of 2009, aged seven and a half, and he died peacefully at home in my arms on the 9th November 2013. He was the best dog a man could have had, and changed my life in so many ways.

Pip's early years as told to me by Sandra

Pip was born on a farm near York, one of a litter of twelve.

We bought Pip because Bob was training with Phoebe (a GSD) and I was just watching, so I fancied trying obedience myself, having only shown dogs in the past. I used to show rough collies, not borders, and had champions during my showing days.

Pip was never used as a stud dog because once used the head can go and as the old saying goes, what they have never had they never miss. He was bought in the main as a pet, but I paid over-the-odds for him because his dad was an obedience champion and I thought with his breeding he should do quite well in obedience. I was not wrong: he was amazing. The shame was that I failed him by not carrying on with him on the obedience circuit.

The GSD would hold no fear for Pip at all, as when having a spat with Phoebe he would just give her the eye and she would start whimpering – end of argument. On the other hand, he would be kind enough to let the little Tibetan spaniel stand on his back and tell him off, only letting her know enough was enough with a snarl and yes when he snarled and lifted his lips he could really look threatening. However, with his lovely nature it was kept well under control.

There's no doubt he would have made an amazing sheepdog; with his strong eye and non-aggressive nature, the sheep would have had no chance. He excelled at training classes when a puppy. Whilst other puppies were still on sit, Pip could do send aways, retrieve, close heelwork, lie down and stay with other dogs walking around him. Needless to say, he soon outgrew the puppy class and was working with the adults at a very early age.

We had to watch him near water or we would hear a plop and he would have slipped in. His fascination for water was cured whilst holidaying on the Mull of Kintyre when he sat down in the sea and a huge wave washed over him. After that he had a bit more respect for the wet stuff. Pip was also very affectionate and given the opportunity you would be wearing him. He would cling on to you with his front legs wrapped around your neck. Pip also loved sticks, but his idea of a stick was the biggest branch he could find. He would run along dragging this and if you were not watching what he was doing you would receive a crack on the back of the legs. We had many bruises to show from this activity!

I am so happy he now lives with you and can show his true talents, teaching other dogs their doggie manners. With an intelligent head like his he needs to be using it. This is why he needs to be with someone who can make the best of his abilities.
X for Pip, Regards, Sandra & Bob

Pip taking a break from a game of fetch.

Ade and Pip

I was looking for a new dog in 2009 and scoured the internet for days. I chanced across Pip and e-mailed Sandra and Bob. I told them I was a specialist dog trainer and that he would be with me every day, working with other dogs. They invited me to meet them and at the end of my visit they offered him to me. I happily accepted, as Pip and I had bonded immediately. Without hesitation he jumped into the back of my car and very quickly became a wonderfully loyal and obedient companion. It felt as though I'd had him from a pup. His papers arrived a little over a week later and it was only then I discovered he had an excellent pedigree.

A child's paddling pool makes a great place for a dog to cool off.

Pip was a handsome dog. But I'm biased.

His father was Obedience Champion Gesviesha Falcon Flyer and he had distinguished grandparents, one an International Supreme Champion and a 1995 Crufts Champion.

To be honest, these accolades don't mean much to me. I like dogs to be dogs and to be off-lead enjoying life, sticking their noses under every bush.

So Warragul Expectations of Glenarran as registered with the Kennel Club© was just Pip to me and he was my No.1 dog. He was brilliant with other dogs, no matter what their problem. He indicated a dog's mental state to me through his body language and by judging his reactions I could then decide on a course of rehabilitation.

He met many dogs with nervous aggression and together we were able to change their behaviour in a very short time. I could not have carried out my job effectively without Pip. For the two years before Buster arrived it was just Ade and Pip, travelling around helping dogs and their owners.

He taught Buster and Jack and they worked brilliantly together as a team. Three breeds, three ages and three different temperaments. Together we could cope with just about anything. In fact by watching Pip I learned so much about dog behaviour that it would be accurate to say he was the teacher and I was his apprentice.

When Pip died in November 2013 it took me a few weeks to gather myself before I could email my clients to tell them of my sad news. I was overwhelmed when over 80 people took the time to write to me and remind me how he had helped their dog and what a difference we had made to their lives, and some just to say how sorry they were to hear of his passing.

Together we DID make a difference and I will never forget him.

He was simply the best.

Buster's Story

I first met Buster the Airedale Terrier in March 2010 and later that year he came to stay *en famille* when his owners went on holiday. In fact we had him for the month of August and quite missed him when he went home, although at the time we lived in quite a small place and we were always tripping over dogs.

Buster had a habit of silently sneaking up behind you in the kitchen. Suddenly his nose would jog your elbow and make you jump out of your skin. He was able to curl up on a tiny rug in the corner and had no issues with Pip at all. He just ignored him and allowed Pip to be in charge.

Adele his owner had taken Buster to puppy classes and he had toilet trained really early and easily, and meekly submitted to grooming, although he appeared to hate it.

Buster didn't like bossy dogs and would floor any dog that tried to be dominant. I recall one incident during a stay with me when a collie cross circled our group for ten minutes, with its tail curled up and stiff and all its hackles up. It went over to Buster and put its head over his back. Within seconds Buster had the dog pinned to the ground. After that it kept a respectful distance. The owner was surprised when I explained that her dog was being dominant aggressive even though she had herself seen it snap and lunge at other dogs when it was on the lead. She didn't think it had a problem!

Buster's owner Adele had heard about me through her sister Katy who needed guidance with her beautiful Labradoodle puppy Bella.

However, Adele had more pressing problems, as Buster had been attacked a couple of times by Labradors when he was only a year old. Since then he would sometimes lunge at other dogs and Adele wasn't sure whether it was play or aggression.

Sometimes it is difficult for owners to tell, as dogs can play very roughly, but also play can get out of hand and develop into a fight. Buster had been attacked both on and off-lead. He was making his own decisions about fight or flight. He didn't seem to like either teenage boys or men, although Adele had two teenage sons of her own. She had once come downstairs to find Buster had pinned one of their friends up against the wall with both paws on the child's shoulders. Buster only seemed to become this protective when Adele was alone with him in the house.

At a boys' rugby match Buster had jumped up at two of the players but this wasn't entirely his fault as some people had encouraged him to jump up previously so Buster thought it was acceptable. However when you are 33 kilos and 24 inches at the shoulder it can be intimidating. Adele had lost a bit of confidence in him and didn't trust his recall, especially when there were sheep around. He tended to bark at the neighbours and visitors and patrolled the garden fence.

Buster could also be incredibly gentle. When Adele's grandma visited, he would sit at her feet with his head resting lightly on her knee. He also seemed to sense she did not have great eyesight or balance and never got in her way.

He was very good on the lead and trotted like a show dog with a loose lead except on the odd occasion when he met a dog he didn't trust.

Buster can follow a scent at speed with his amazing sense of smell.

Isn't this what you call a Bench Press?

Sun, sea, sand and me. What more could a human want?

Adele's Goals for Buster

- Wants to know if the dog is aggressive, or just playful
- Easy to walk on lead with no lunging or barking
- Better recall (at present no control if sheep are around)
- Barking at the neighbours and visitors stopped
- Patrolling of the fence curtailed
- To be sociable with sons' friends
- Stop jumping up

My first meeting with Buster was out on the street in neutral territory. Pip's tail flagged up a warning, but after a small initial lunge Buster stood still. Pip lost interest in Buster, his tail went down and he soon found a piece of wood to play fetch. I took Buster's lead, made one correction with a quick snap tug and he sat down. Adele was surprised at Buster obeying a stranger so quickly.

Firstly Pip had indicated that Buster was no threat by his body language. Buster was just unsure about certain dogs and decided to get in first after being attacked a couple of times. It is very common for dogs that have been attacked when young to go into nervous aggressive self defence mode as they get older and more able to stick up for themselves.

We were soon able to let Buster and Pip off lead together. Pip as usual focused on a stick and Buster trotted along, letting his nose lead him. We did some recall exercises and talked about how to control Buster and get his confidence and also worked through each of his problems.

Little did I know then what an important part of my team and my life Buster would turn out to be.

A year passed and out of the blue I had a call from Adele. Her work situation had changed and it would mean Buster being alone throughout the day and she didn't feel it would be fair on him. After much soul-searching and many tears from all the family who loved Buster she asked if I would like to have him. I didn't hesitate to accept her offer. I missed the big curly terrier trotting majestically around the park, drawing attention from everyone who saw him and thought him the perfect addition to my pack. Adele was right that he trotted like a show dog and he would break into a joyful canter if I could entice him into playing a game of chase.

Four years later and Buster's turned into a great dog. He loves his bed and spends a lot of the time snoozing when he can. He only gets up when he hears the other two dogs getting excited before their walk. On the odd occasion that he needs to go out in the night he will barge our bedroom door open with a thump and stick his nose in my face. As soon as I get up he trots into the kitchen and stares at the back door handle.

When Buster is hungry he will do a little front paw dance in front of me, then sit and paw my leg. Usually he uses one paw, sometimes if he is really hungry he will put both paws on my leg and stare at me as if to say: look here stupid, I need feeding NOW! Gimme gimme! He will add in a little throaty soft bark just to let me know I am failing in my duties as a responsible dog owner.

Jack on the other hand will bounce up and down on the spot and run into the kitchen barking, and then spin around in excitement.

If I am in the office all day and I haven't fed them by lunchtime – they let me know.

Now he is 10 years old, Buster will sometimes decide that another lap of the field is too much trouble, and he sits by the cricket square and watches the rest of us get our exercise. He may then deign to join us when we get close to him again. He is a constant source of amusement to the regulars on our park who almost break into applause if he breaks into anything more than a trot. He is known as Mr. Cool and certainly lives up to his name. He puts a smile on the face of everyone he meets and doesn't like to get his paws muddy. Adele told me he walked around mud and I didn't quite believe her, but he picks his way over the ground and is certainly cleaner than the other two when we get back from a walk.

He is great with other dogs because he stays calm all the time and this seems to help dogs with aggression or nervous problems. If he has to meet aggressive dogs during our work together he will ignore them. I can then correct the other dog and get them under control much more quickly than any other method.

Airedales don't seem to be as popular as they once were but they are a lovely breed, as with any dog the behaviour is down to the training and the owners.

Buster is certainly one of the most popular dogs around, he got more birthday greetings than I did on Facebook this year!

Buster, Pip and Jack have probably met more badly-behaved dogs than any other dogs in history and new addition Fliss is learning quickly.

To quote Adele when I asked her to tell me Buster's story:-

I don't think I will ever have another dog – there will never be another Buster.

Well, there will always be dogs in my life but I agree on one thing, there will never be another Buster.

Shortly after his eleventh birthday Buster was diagnosed with lymphoma, a cancer of the white blood cells. Ten days later, after his condition deteriorated, he was put to sleep to stop any further suffering. He will always live on in our hearts.

I need a hug

A lot of dogs are frightened of fireworks and although Buster doesn't make a big fuss about it he does like to be as close as possible to us. Our dogs are not usually allowed on the sofas but Buster decided that when frightened the best place was to be as close to Elaine as possible. I rushed to get the camera to record it for posterity

Jack's story

Jack is a black Cocker Spaniel. He has a distinguished pedigree, a Swedish father and a multiple Show Champion mother. He was known as Jigsaw and first came to my attention in February 2012 when he was 15 months old and still an entire male. He had become very possessive over food, chews and bones and the odd flip-flop. He had chewed a door mat and some wooden kitchen chairs to the point of destruction. He pulled on the lead and jumped on people and would try to jump up on the worktops to steal food.

He slept in the utility room and scratched and whimpered at the door every morning from 7am to be let in.

His owner had told him off for growling at him and Jack had bitten his hand quite deeply, requiring a visit to A&E.

The local vet put them in contact with me and I went to meet them to sort out this feisty little Cocker.

I had never seen a set of Windsor dining chairs and table in such a state.

They looked as if a family of beavers had moved in and enjoyed a long lunch. It was obvious that Jigsaw was on borrowed time.

I worked with Jigsaw, confronted all his bad habits and showed his owners how to correct him and avoid any triggers to his aggression. Jigsaw didn't bite me and showed the proper respect throughout the session. The owners appeared happy and seemed to understand what they needed to do. I heard nothing for several weeks, which made me think – as I always do – that all was well and the dog was behaving.

It was the busy period after Christmas and New Year when people have had enough of bad behaviour over the holidays and someone has said "Get that dog sorted out or its going!"

One day the phone rang. It was Jigsaw's owner, Mike. Jigsaw had growled and snapped menacingly from the sofa at Matthew their adult son. Mike's wife was understandably scared as she had been sitting on the sofa next to Jigsaw at the time. She had become frightened to be alone with him. Mike told me Jigsaw could not be rehomed because Rescue Centres won't take dogs that have become aggressive to humans.

To try to cure his aggressive behaviour, Jigsaw had been castrated; this is commonly advocated in the hope that it will sort out aggression. Some hope.

I would never advise anyone to do this to a dog to cure aggression. I have had experience of several dogs that have become even more aggressive after the operation.

Aggressive dogs need the correct training – not surgery.

When you think about it, every animal in its natural surroundings would be entire, that is, not neutered and they seem to be able to work things out in the pack or herd as nature intended. It is only humans who mess up their heads and then neuter them to try to solve the problem.

Jack in full flow on the beach making sure the seagulls stayed aloft

I was asked if I knew anyone who would take Jigsaw, as the alternative was euthanasia.

I immediately said I would – I didn't want him put down and I was confident he could be fixed fairly quickly. I then had to send a grovelling text to my girlfriend to ask her to squeeze another dog into our small bungalow.

"We'll discuss it tonight" came the reply…

Jack. The Black Prince strutting his stuff

That evening Elaine asked the big question. "Can you fix him?"

"Yes, of course" I said, "it should only take a couple of weeks."

At the time Elaine was going through some fairly serious medical treatment which was affecting her immune system.

"You've got a week" she said, "and if he bites me, he's gone."

No pressure then!

Time for a little breather. Fancy a dip anyone?

Jigsaw left his owners' house and arrived at mine with a new name. I couldn't see myself shouting "Jigsaw" as I called to him on the playing field, so he became Black Jack as his coat was a thick shiny black and he had a dark side to him, an aggressive controlling streak which nearly got him killed. His eyes were also very dark: when he challenged you, you couldn't see any white, just these menacing, staring deep brown orbs.

Jack soon learned that everything in my house belongs to *me*. No *dog* food, *dog* toys or *dog* beds. Everything is *mine* until I give it to the dogs or allow them to use it.

It is part of my cure for possessive aggression.

Jack was possessive over his bed, food and toys and attempted to claim my sofa as well by standing on it and growling and snapping at me.

A quick slap with a sofa cushion bettered his threat[1] and he scuttled into a corner of the room. I followed him to enforce my ranking in the pack. As I crouched down over him and he growled at me, I heard another growl behind me and looked over my shoulder to see Pip giving him the full snarling, teeth-bared threat. My dog was backing me up!

Jack was of course desperate to join the pack in the house. Each time he misbehaved, however, he was chased out of the house and excluded.

I had adapted and adopted the chase after I had seen it work with horses, and found out that it works with dogs too. It simulates an 'attack' from a senior-ranked dog to discipline a junior dog for some misdemeanour. I have studied and adapted some Horse Whisperer methods, which have allowed me to achieve quick results.

The attack doesn't even touch the dog: the idea is to psychologically drive him away from the pack. He cannot enjoy the comfort, socialisation and security that a pack affords UNLESS he conforms to the unwritten rules and takes his place in the pecking order. Whenever he was allowed back into the house he would approach with head low and a low tail wag. He was giving me visual signals of his submission. I would not stroke him.

His reward was to be allowed in our personal space and our den.

He soon learned that he was the lowest-ranked, and deferred to the other two dogs. I told Elaine not to touch him at all even if he came up for some fuss. He could turn and bite in a moment and I could not risk that.

For two weeks we ignored him and made him stay out of our personal space. I did not handle him, apart from putting a lead on him and drying his paws. I did not approach him to put his lead on. He had to come to me, in a submissive manner, a totally different thing to me going into HIS personal space. In the evening he would growl at me if I leaned over his bed to draw the curtains. I made sure he was regularly tipped out of his bed if he did this, and I would then kneel on the bed to claim it as mine. On a couple of occasions he even spent the night outside in the lean-to conservatory, a dilapidated structure which was barely weatherproof and without heat. Fortunately for Jack, he has an extremely thick and long coat which gives him perfect insulation, vital against those cold March nights. I found that when I opened the door in the morning he would vacate his bed and go and stand a respectful distance away from me until I gave him the signal to enter the house.

He wasn't hurt in the slightest[1]

I used the cushion to shock and surprise him and to distract and correct. His bite threat signals were ignored so he went into flight mode and then showed submission in the corner of the room

I considered that I was being hard on him to save his life.

I had taken on a dog which was clearly dangerous. One of his favourite tricks with his previous owners was to steal some tissue out of the waste paper basket, take it under the stairs, shred it and then growl and snap at anyone who happened to walk by.

I had to act quickly to protect Elaine from a possible bite and infection and I did not want to be bitten myself either. I have had plenty of dog bites over the years and they don't get any less painful…

Jack changed his behaviour. He learned from me and my other dogs regularly put him in his place. Pip in particular only tolerated him at best but even so he would back Jack up if he was threatened by another dog. Pip even fought another dog that had bitten Jack.

Only once has Jack put his teeth on me. One evening he came up to me while I was watching TV and put his head on my knee. As soon as I started stroking his head he started growling at me and put his teeth on my hand, not biting but taking it into his mouth, while staring and growling. I leaned forward and realised I hadn't noticed he had dropped a half-eaten rawhide chew at my feet. I removed my hand slowly and stood up, moving him away from the chew with my legs. I stood over the chew, picked it up when he backed away and then told him to get out of the room.

Jack has never bitten anyone since. I would trust him with anyone. He has turned out to be a fantastic little dog and a great character.

He doesn't know how close he came to death.

Fliss's story

Fliss is a Border Collie and I first saw her in January of 2014 when she was just over two years old. I was quite shocked when I met her as the resemblance to Pip was quite striking at first glance. Having lost Pip in November of 2013 I was still feeling raw with grief.

Fliss was a lot smaller than Pip and had many faults. She had been a gift for a young boy who had lost interest in her and she ended up spending all of her time with his elderly grandmother. At one point Fliss had weighed 27kg so had been put on a diet to reduce her weight. It didn't help that she got very little exercise and even her outings into the back garden had to be curtailed as she was constantly barking at birds and squirrels and annoying the neighbours.

Fliss ears pricked, ready to play. Always ready to play!

Just time to cool my tummy before we start all over again

Fliss rarely strays more than 30 yards away from me. She's always looking over her shoulder

She would jump up and scratch at the door, guard at the front door and bark at anything going past, and she was a horrendous puller on the extendable lead they used.

What I didn't know was that she also had a fear of traffic and would try to bolt if a car came close to her. Several times she almost yanked my arm off when she took me by surprise. Her constant licking was annoying and she was a persistent attention seeker. Because of her lack of exercise and mental stimulation she would pace around for hours at a time. She had a bad case of cabin fever.

I worked with her and could see she was very willing to learn but her situation did not lend itself to there being a satisfactory outcome for everybody. At the end of the session I offered to take her if they felt she might benefit from more exercise, attention and training. A few days later they called and I collected her soon after.

Within an hour I took her to the park with Jack and Buster and let her off-lead. I wanted to see if she would come back when called. She bounded off with Jack and when she got about 40 metres away I whistled and she came straight back and sat in front of me. I was quite impressed.

She had obviously had some training. The rest of the faults are slowly being eliminated although fear of traffic is never a short term fix. The fear is something she will have to overcome by seeing more and more traffic and realising it is not going to harm her and that she will be safe standing next to me.

When working, she reacts to aggressive dogs which is good as Jack and Buster tend to go into avoidance straight away. Fliss will snarl and bark back at a dog displaying anti-social body language. I don't know whether it is a collie thing but Pip did the same thing. He was brilliant at making a dog back down and start to behave. Fliss is also very good at backing me up when I barge a dog for misbehaving which proves what I do must make sense to the dogs. In time she will be a good dog, but it is so frustrating that I can usually get a dog to stop pulling in about 10 minutes but her fear of traffic overwhelms her and she dives to the floor and scrabbles up the street. In the park she walks beautifully to heel and will sit and stay and recall very well. I really need to spend a little more time training my own dogs instead of everyone else's!

CHAPTER 2
It's a dog's life

Dogs can only behave like dogs. Dogs do not deliberately set out to misbehave or to upset their owners.

Let's consider a dog's life from the dog's point of view.

A young dog is born in a litter of six. It has a happy life for its first 12 weeks, with its mother and brothers and sisters, learning how to be a dog like them. Suddenly it is plucked from its family and forcibly fostered out to humans who try to make it do certain things that are at odds with its natural development. It is fussed over and cuddled and stroked for hours because it is so cute and cuddly. They call it Woody.

Woody naturally keeps close to his new owner because of all the attention he is getting, but is made to sleep alone at night. He cries out for company, feels stressed and can't control his bowel movements yet; if he makes a mess this is met with harsh words and sometimes punishment from the owner who does not want to clear up dog mess first thing in the morning.

The human gives Woody his food and then takes it away after a minute or two to 'stop him being possessive over food'. Woody starts to wolf his food down and snaps at the owner the next time the food is taken away.

The owner puts a collar around Woody's neck. He either drags the dog around, yanking on the lead and saying **"heel heel heel"** or the dog pulls so hard it starts to choke itself. The human can't understand why the dog is pulling. Woody does not understand why he has a rope around his neck or why he has to drag around the slow lump of lard on the other end of the lead when he wants to investigate a new scent or meet another dog. He barks and lunges towards the other dog because he is so excited at seeing one of his own kind and wants to play. His owner drags him away because he feels Woody is being aggressive.

Woody jumps up to greet his owner. He has muddy paws. The owner gets annoyed and pushes the dog off. Woody thinks it is a game. He keeps jumping up and starts to mouth and nip the arm of the owner as well. The human starts shouting at him as he pushes the dog off with his hands. The dog thinks this is a great game and gets excited and bites harder. Woody eventually draws blood.

Woody is in the park and runs over to greet another dog, which is on a lead. The other dog's human pulls his dog close to him and starts shouting at Woody. Woody thinks they are both excited to see him and keeps running around barking at the dog and its owner. It's great fun! Let's play! Then his owner runs up and joins in the fuss by making his own funny barking noises. Luckily Woody does not understand swear words.

The high energy of Spaniels often drive their owners to re-home

Large Breeds dogs like Tunoo the Malamute can become difficult to handle because of their sheer size

Popular dogs such as German Shepherds often have rescue centres devoted to the breed. This one clearly loves the water!

Now Woody is never let off the lead or allowed to meet other dogs and only gets 20 minutes exercise because he pulls so hard. He goes out late at night with his owner so that he is unlikely to meet other dogs. His owner grows to hate taking him for a walk and having to avoid other people.

Woody is unsure of what to do when strangers come into the house. He usually barks at strangers and dogs that approach the house; they walk off, so he must be a great guard dog. He never gets told off for barking; in fact the humans join in and start barking **"shut up"** loudly, so Woody thinks he is in charge, he leads and they follow don't you see? When people come into the house he tries to warn them off, but his owner puts him in the kitchen.

Woody becomes very frustrated and keeps barking to be let out. He gets so excited that if they let him out he runs around barking and jumping all over the furniture and people and going crazy with excitement. He can't resist having a little nip at someone in play, as he would with his siblings.

Later that night Woody keeps his head down as his owners start barking loudly at each other. The man puts Woody's lead on. Woody expects a walk before bedtime as usual but instead is put into the back of the car.

As dawn breaks Woody finds himself tied to the gate of the rescue centre.

His owner is nowhere to be seen.

Everything Woody has done has been entirely natural, instinctive and predictable to a dog.

This sort of scenario is a very common one; I hear similar stories from people every week about their new rescue dogs that were found as strays, abandoned or handed in because of family problems.

The dogs pictured on this page were not all from rescues but they all had some behavioural problems which needed addressing.

URBAN MYTH

YOU SHOULD ALWAYS MAKE SURE YOU WIN THE TUG GAME.

WRONG!

I played tug with my collie Pip almost every day for years. Every day I would let him win. I would just let go of the rope and he would bring it straight back with his tail wagging wanting to play again. He would assume a play bow. That is a signal for play not competition.

Tug is a GAME. It should not be seen as a contest for ranking.

Challenge signals are very different from play signals and tug is a very good way to direct your puppy's play bites onto something you don't mind him biting.

I always advise clients against play fighting with the hands because you are teaching your puppy it is okay to put their teeth on your hands. This can lead to biting/mouthing problems very quickly.

YOU SHOULD NEVER PLAY TUG WITH YOUR DOG AS IT WILL MAKE IT AGGRESSIVE.

WRONG!

Tug is a very natural game for dogs and when they tire of it they stop playing. So you can act just like a dog and when you have had enough turn and walk away to indicate play is over.

If you think your dog is getting too intense during the game you finish it.

Dogs may growl during the game. This does not mean they are getting aggressive but if you feel unsure then use your discretion and end the game.

You can also raise your chin in the air and look away to indicate you are not interested at all.

You just need to use your common sense and a bit of gut instinct occasionally.

CHAPTER 3
The General and the Sentry

How to get your dog
to sit and stay in two
minutes or less.

This exercise is very
powerful and it really
works. It doesn't take
weeks of training.
It literally takes minutes.

I call it the General and the Sentry because I use it with dogs that are hard to control when callers come to the front door. The Sentry (the dog) lets the General (the owner) know that someone is at the front door. The General then sends him back to his Sentry post while he deals with whatever is on the other side of the door.

The psychology behind it
The General and the Sentry is a threat/challenge exercise which a dog understands because it uses the same technique on other dogs and humans. Let us say a dog growls at you. This is a warning: it wants a bit of personal space and is threatening you to get it.

Your natural reaction is to move away. It will already be staring at you, another warning which we as humans don't usually recognise as a warning. Some people refer to it as a dog 'giving you the eye'.

It may then growl if you move into its personal space. Move any closer and it may start to curl its lip and snarl or bark or you may even get a mock charge. It may advance towards you, aggressively barking to try and make you back off. I often see small dogs doing a mock charge to other dogs or humans, especially if they are backed into a confined space.

If you continue to ignore all these warnings, it may bite you to make you go away.

Each warning becomes progressively louder and more aggressive because the dog wants you to move away and give it space, but the point is that the dog does not really want to bite you or fight you.

The warnings are there to avoid a fight.

Most of it is bravado. It's their way of saying: "I don't like the look of you and I see you as a possible threat and you are entering my personal space. I am warning you that I will protect myself but if you move away everything will be okay."

You can control the dog by using the same technique, somewhat adapted; you can establish a higher ranking and become its pack leader.

It is all about **controlling space**.
Here's how…

Block, barge, bark and stare.

Here's Molly looking for the next signal

Molly is totally focused on her owner

Harvey paying full attention

Block

1 Firstly I use a narrow hallway to allow me to block the dog's movement easily. If it tries to squeeze past me I use my legs to block it or trap its head against the wall. A trapped dog will always pull back which is what I want it to do.

2 I keep my hands behind me so the dog knows it is not a game. Hands are fun, fuss and food to a dog. I keep my hands out of the way so that the dog can focus on eye contact and not be distracted by hand movements. Hand signals may be introduced at a later date.

Barge

1 I nudge the dog back to the end of the hall using my legs, knees or shins.

2 I keep my feet on the floor and shuffle as I barge the dog back as I wouldn't want anyone to think I am kicking their dog. It is a barge or a nudge only. I call it the penguin shuffle!

3 When the dog is trapped at the end of the hallway it will either sit down and look at you or stand sideways on to you, with its head and tail lowered. These signals are indicating submission. Yes, sitting down is a submissive signal.

4 When the dog is stationary, make eye contact and start to move back, lowering your head slightly and staring at the dog: these are both threat signals to a dog.

Bark

1 If the dog starts to move towards me I bark out a loud "A" and take a quick step towards the dog. The reasons I use the "A" are: It is the first letter of the alphabet and easy for a human to remember!

2 It sounds very much like "STAY".

3 The hard "A" sound makes your voice drop to a lower register so it sounds more like a warning/threatening bark. High tones are more exciting to a dog so if you use an "ah ah" or that ridiculous "watch me" signal it can create excitement and the dog naturally wants to come to you. A good "A" bark can stop a dog in its tracks.

4 When I take a quick step towards the dog, it will probably interpret it as a mock charge, another threat signal.

Stare

1   As I back away from the dog to the other end of the hallway I lower my head slightly and stare at the dog. These are threat signals. I am saying to the dog, keep out of my space until I signal to you that you can approach me.

2   I call it THE PARENT STARE because everyone knows the parent stare.

Every child recognises the parent stare. Teachers use it as well.

The body remains motionless. The head slightly lowers and the eyes bore into you in a threatening manner. The lips are slightly drawn back and the teeth are bared slightly. The voice drops and then… your mother uses your FULL NAME!!!

Oh crikey are YOU in trouble!

It works with dogs as well as children. In fact, several teachers have told me there are many similarities between training children and dogs.

The release

1   When the dog has stayed for between 10 and 20 seconds I lower my gaze, bring my hands out in front of me and crouch down a little saying "come on then" or something similar in a high welcoming voice.

2   Usually the dog will come bounding towards me at full speed for a fuss. Nervous dogs will approach with low head and wagging tail and curved body (like a cat) to show submission and fearful dogs may just creep forward or stay there until I actually walk away.

If you have done this correctly you have managed to get your dog to sit, stay and come in under two minutes without a command or a treat. You have done it by using a dog technique on a dog. That is why the dog understands it. Congratulations.

Try blocking your dog into any corner of a room and repeat. You can use this method anywhere in the house to keep your dog out of your personal space. This control of space makes the dog regard you as a higher rank.

Use the method at the front door as follows. Let your dog settle down somewhere away from the front door or get someone to distract it.

1   Pretend there is a caller. Move to the front door and knock on the door from the inside. The dog will usually rush to the door, barking.

2   After allowing the dog to get to the door you must get between it and the door by using your legs to move it away from the door. Open the door an inch and ask your imaginary caller to wait for a minute.

3   Use your knees and shins to move the dog away from the door to the far end of the hall, where you will make it stay by blocking.

4   Walk backwards to the door and keep staring at the dog. If it moves, block it or use the mock charge.

5 Make sure when you open the door that you are still staring at the dog. Some dogs will read looking away as an invitation to move into your space again. It does not mean the dog has done something wrong. It means you changed your signals and the dog reacted to it.

6 Have a little chat with your imaginary caller and then close the door and release the dog. Usually he'll come a-running.

After a couple of attempts ask a friend to go away from the house for a minute and then return and ring the bell.

The dog can see what is going on at all times and is not excluded from the process but because you are controlling the situation the excitement level is reduced to almost nothing after a few practices.

It is very important that you **maintain eye contact** with the dog throughout this exercise. The stare is really important. I often see dogs that bark at the door and won't stop for 10 minutes or more. This method takes about 45 minutes to teach the owner and the barking then stops after three or four barks. Yes, 45 minutes, sometimes less.

The technique changes the way your dog regards you. You are recognised as being a higher rank. By using your legs to make the dog move out of your space it understands that you mean business, you are barging it out of your way in effect.

If you use hands to block or pull a dog it can turn into a game. In fact, if you use a lead or grab the dog by the collar to move it you are simply getting into a test of physical strength not a psychological battle of wills.

You are not creating fear.

You are creating respect because when released the dog is happy to come to you. A dog that is afraid would run away or bite you.

It is one of the core techniques I use on every dog I train and my clients are absolutely amazed at the quick results they get with their dogs which ignored them previously.

So remember: **BLOCK, BARGE, BARK** and **STARE**.

Client review

**All I can say is WOW.
I would recommend Ade to anyone.**

My Bertha had a problem with people and dogs, and you entered at your own risk coming into the house.

Ade taught me how to get control of my house back and deal with Bertha. I have put this into practice and she now allows people to enter and although there is still some barking she is coming along a treat :) As for her aggression towards dogs once again Ade taught me what to do and how to handle her when walking, we even went out for a walk with his three dogs and that's never happened before.

This is still work in progress but it's amazing how far she has come since Ade came to help me. I would highly recommend Ade and his wonderful tolerant dogs. Can't thank them enough. *Joanne Walton*

THE GENERAL AND THE SENTRY

BLOCK
BARGE
BARK
STARE
RELEASE

BY USING THIS METHOD YOU CONTROL A DOG'S MOVEMENT AND CREATE RESPECT – NOT FEAR.

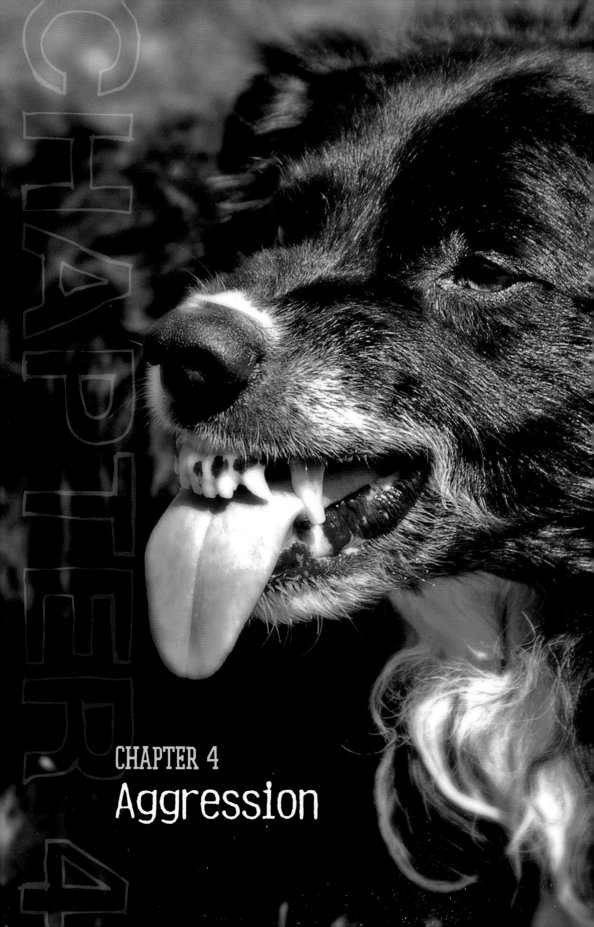

CHAPTER 4
Aggression

Dog-on-dog aggression is a fairly common problem.

A lot of owners are not certain whether their dog is aggressive or not.

Most decide to be better safe than sorry and isolate their dogs, staying away from parks and open spaces and crossing the road if they see a dog approaching or walking their pet late at night and early in the morning.

A lot of misleading information is available to people in the form of books, DVDs or the internet. All well-intentioned but the methods don't work. The two main methods they advocate are shown below.

1   **Distract** with a treat or a toy and then praise and reward the dog when it does not show aggression. To my way of thinking you are not correcting the dog for bad behaviour. You are simply distracting it.
    The dog does not know its behaviour is unacceptable and it is being rewarded for doing nothing. In fact you can be rewarding a dog that is still planning its next attack.

    Where is the logic in that? It is a very slow method and may not get any permanent results.

2   **Move the dog away from another dog** if it shows any aggression, and then keep coming nearer *ad infinitum* until the dog is calm. Again, the dog remains unaware that its behaviour is unacceptable

and many will lunge again and again. It is just reacting instinctively.

I do not use either of these methods. They are quite pointless and a waste of valuable time. The aim is to stop the bad behaviour permanently and I believe the dog needs to be corrected in a way it understands.

Here is my tried and tested method of curing dog aggression – quickly.

1   Assessment

2   Confrontation

3   Avoidance and submission

4   Joining up

5   Socialisation

Assessment

It helps if I know a dog's history; unfortunately, the past of some rescue dogs is purposely omitted or modified by previous owners so that it can be re-homed.

I ask a lot of questions:

1   Does it lunge, bark, snarl or snap?

2   Does it get on with any dogs at all?

3   When did it start and has it got worse over time?

4   Has the dog ever been attacked by another dog or dogs when younger?

This is important, because a large proportion of the dog aggression cases I see are rooted in an attack at a young age by an older dog. The dog may have been re-homed three or four times since then, so owners don't always know the truth.

I will also assess **how the owner regards the dog** and **how obedient the dog is in the home**. The owner may have received the dog in a poor condition. Many, because they feel sorry for it, try to make up for its maltreatment by treating it with kid gloves. This is a big mistake. Dogs feel and behave far better if you **set the rules**, make them clear and give the dog a leader to follow.

I ask the owner to get the dog to sit and stay in any place in the house. The dog will usually sit for three seconds if at all and then move. If it does not take the owner seriously inside the house, why would it follow them as leader anywhere else?

I will teach the owners how to use the blocking and threat/challenge technique to take control in the house. (See chapter titled General and Sentry). This usually takes 45 minutes to an hour in total.

Next I will show them how to get control of the dog with the slip lead, and **be in charge of the walk**. I spend 20-30 minutes doing this.

By now I have a much better understanding and control of the dog and it is responding to my visual and verbal commands.

Confrontation and correction

I have to assess how aggressive the dog really is before I can fix it. This is where my own dogs play their part.

Pip was absolutely brilliant with other dogs and told me by his body language if a dog was aggressive or just over-excited. Since Pip died I bring out Buster first because I know he will be very calm and ignore the other dog. Fliss the collie is relatively new to the business and is quite reactive to dogs that are unbalanced so I leave her until later.

I ask the owner to keep a good grip on the leash without keeping it taut and to stand in an area which is big enough to contain a circle with a radius of about four metres: this is to keep each dog a safe distance from the other.

Buster is on the lead so that I can see his reaction to the other dog. He will usually keep away from the other dog if it is showing signs of aggression or over-excitement. He will look at the dog to read its body language and if he detects any sign of unbalance he will ignore it.

Most of the dogs I see I would describe as being isolated by their owners from other dogs. Their barking, lunging and snapping has made them forget their dog manners and instead they react in a nervous, aggressive way because they are not used to being in other dogs' company. They are not all spoiling for a fight. Most of their fuss and display is bravado. They just need reminding of their manners, and lots of socialisation.

I take the problem dog from the owner and ask them to hold Buster in the centre of the circle by his lead, which is a metre and a half long. I tell them to allow him its full length so he can move around them if he wants to keep an eye on the other dog.

I walk the dog around Buster in a circle at a distance of three or four metres. If the dog lunges, I will pull the head up and immediately barge it on the top of the front shoulder near the neck and give a short, sharp "A" bark. Then I will make eye contact with it, stare and lower my head. The dog understands these corrections and threats **immediately** as we have already used them in the house.

It will stop lunging, cower down slightly with a low head and tail to show submission and look away. This is avoidance.

In dog language I have said this:

"I have already shown you that I am a senior rank in the pack by the exercises in the house and on the lead.

This dog Buster is in my pack and under my protection. If you display any aggression towards him I will attack you and he may join in. I am much bigger and stronger than you as I have just shown you by the barge on your neck. So – you have a choice. Fight me and Buster, or go into avoidance."

The barge on top of the neck is to simulate what senior dogs do to show dominance. I am trying to simulate a dog jumping onto the back of another dog and biting its neck to put it in its place without actually doing any jumping or biting. Dominance is a nasty word in a lot of training circles, so I could say I am of senior rank in the pack.

It does not harm the dog in any way and the dog shows a lot more respect afterwards.

Avoidance

Dogs have several choices when they meet other dogs. They can:

1   Meet and greet in a friendly way

2   Meet, but growl and maybe snap to warn the other dog to keep its distance

3   Give lots of threat signals such as growling, barking and lunging to make the other dog stay well away

4   Go straight into attack

5   Run away

6   Show calm, submissive avoidance

I want to teach the dog in Category 2, 3 and 4 to go into calm submissive avoidance first and then socialise it safely with other dogs.

After I have corrected the dog, it understands that the nervous aggression choice is unacceptable, so it has no choice but to go into avoidance. We have removed the flight option (Option 5) because we have it on a lead.

Next, I walk the dog around Buster and correct any staring. Staring is a threat signal and Buster will ignore it and leave the correcting to me. I correct the dog with a sharp **"Leave it!"** and a snap tug on the lead. Within minutes the dog will be walking around Buster and looking away, and also moving away from him rather than trying to lunge towards him and snap. I keep as loose a lead as possible, so that there is no tension on the lead from me.

When I am satisfied the owner understands what has happened, I allow them to take control of their dog and start the process again from a distance of four metres, gradually reducing the radius of the circle but allowing the dog to keep its distance from Buster by using the full length of the lead.

As soon as the dog's body language changes from aggression to avoidance, Buster will relax and lie down, but he will keep a watchful eye on it as it is walked around him. Often the previously aggressive dog will try to move AWAY from Buster to give him some personal space.

People are amazed how quickly their dog's behaviour changes from screaming hysterics to good manners in the space of 20 minutes.

Putting on the pressure
The next stage is to put the dog under a bit of pressure by introducing my two other dogs: Jack, my Cocker Spaniel and Fliss, a young female collie. I repeat the exercise with three dogs walking around the other dog, watching the signs, taking corrective action if necessary and teaching the owner the importance of the **timing** and **intensity** of the correction. Correct the dog when it starts staring and you pre-empt the lunge – you read your dog's mind, in effect, and thus do not allow its behaviour to escalate.

If a dog is staring at one of my dogs, it is already planning an attack, waiting for the other dog to come within range. A pre-emptive correction stops the aggression before it happens.

Soon the dog is calm and submissive and all my dogs usually ignore it, facing the other way and avoiding eye contact.

Joining up

Now the dog has stopped its aggressive behaviour and the owner has some control I invite the dog to join my pack. Very simply, we go for a walk.

It's not quite as simple as that, of course.

I will ask the owner to walk **behind** my dogs, so that there is no eye contact. It also gives the other dog, maybe for the first time in ages, a chance to start to sniff and walk in a group without any confrontation.

As soon as I see the dog's nose start to twitch, I know I am getting somewhere. Soon it will start to pick up my dogs' calm demeanour, and relax. After a few minutes of this, I will bring the new dog to the front of the group to see how it reacts to strange dogs walking behind it. A nervous dog may look around a lot to start off with, to see where my dogs are but again, they pick up the body language, relax and start to behave normally. Soon they start to sniff the bushes and lamp posts as we pass.

Now I increase the pressure by surrounding it on three sides with my dogs, one behind it and one to each side. I have often had an owner walking all four dogs together within 30 minutes. It is not unusual for some owners to become quite emotional seeing their dog behaving sensibly for the first time.

I always carry tissues…

If the dog has a problem with other dogs in the neighbourhood I will deliberately walk past the houses where the dogs live and get it to stand calmly on the pavement outside. I do not make it sit down, unless it wants to. Forcing a dog to sit down is irrelevant in my opinion and may make a dog more nervous, as you are forcing it into a submissive position; however, you are in charge and your demand that it shows calm submissive behaviour is the cure.

I will correct the dog if it shows any signs of retaliation and it will go into avoidance and ignore the other dog. The barking at the neighbours' gate soon stops after it gets no reaction: all four dogs are telling it **"yes, we can hear you but we're not bothered about you. We are going to ignore you so you might as well shut up and go away, you plonker."**

Socialisation

We are nearly there.

I have to decide whether the client's dog can be allowed off-lead with my dogs, either in the park or in a confined area such as a back garden. I will have been assessing the dog over the previous two hours, and noted how my dogs are reacting to it.

If I see good signs from all the dogs, I allow them to mingle freely. The few dogs I am still not sure of will be muzzled and kept on a loose lead to start with, to protect my own. I will shadow the dog for five or 10 minutes, always keeping within a few metres of it so I can check for any signals that indicate aggression and immediately step in if I need to. I then allow my dogs to do their work and correct the dog if necessary. Each has a role to play. They are three different breeds, three different sizes and temperaments. They also have a ranking between them.

Buster will normally go into avoidance straight away, facing the other way, unless a dog wants to pick a fight. Then he puts them in their place pretty quickly.

Younger dogs will want to play with Jack, who will join in cheerfully. If, however, a dog tries to pick on him, and he barks and snaps in a certain way, Fliss will immediately rush in to threaten an attack. I will be close behind, backing up both dogs and correcting with vocal commands and a barge if necessary. We indicate to the other dog that if it takes on one of us, it takes on all of us. Dogs can count, and their survival instinct is strong, so they choose to change their behaviour rather than take on our pack.

By putting a dog in a pack scenario I use its survival instinct to change their behaviour. It works.

Nine times out of ten the dog will be off-lead with my dogs if they have indicated to me that they are comfortable with the other dog. Sometimes the dog is muzzled for all our safety. Sometimes I just won't risk letting a dog near my dogs until it has learned some manners.

The whole process usually takes just under three hours

It works quickly because I communicate with a dog so that it understands and reacts instantly, as it would to signals from other dogs.

I don't expect dogs to understand English, so I do my level best to speak their language which is mostly sign language if you think about it.

The biggest problem my clients face after this session is finding enough people who will walk their dog with them, as they have probably earned a reputation in their neighbourhood as the couple with a vicious dog.

My techniques are all tried and tested and they work.

Most importantly none of the dogs suffers in any way.

I communicate with them firmly and clearly in ways they understand; I treat them how they would be treated in the wild. And talking of treats, I don't use them.

My methods are not found in any training manual I have seen, but I can confidently say that they result in calmer, happier and more confident dogs – and owners. My results – and my clients – speak for themselves.

Dog owners who come to me will have tried the conventional routes – dog training classes, stuffing their animal with treats, individual trainers with their instructions to do weird and wacky things like wrapping a dog up in bandages or using calming scent dispensers, distraction techniques or simply blaming the owners. These will all have failed. I am quite literally their last resort.

Aggressive dog story

Sarah Catton tells the story of Tammy the German Shepherd
We have always had rescue dogs and are used to their quirky nature. This time we took in Kita and Tammy, two German Shepherds that had been found abandoned in a pub. Kita, the elder dog, has always been an amazing dog. She settled quickly and we love her dearly.

The younger, Tammy, was supposed to be the sweetheart of the two, but this did not turn out to be the case!

I remember our first walk very well.

As soon as we got to the middle of the drive she exploded into whines, barks, frenzied noises, jumping and pulling on the lead! We thought it was just a case of her wanting to let off steam! When we got to the park and let her off the lead, we watched aghast as she attacked every other dog within a five-mile radius.

We knew we were in trouble!

The scariest thing was, she just needed to be outdoors with or without another dog to get into this state. In the house she was as good as gold. It usually takes a while for rescue dogs to adjust and settle, sometimes as long as a year, and we thought that this was Tammy's problem. It wasn't!

We took to walking them both at 10 o'clock at night to avoid all the other dog walkers in the park. Unfortunately this didn't stop the explosion of noise on the way to the park but there was nothing we could do to silence her – our poor neighbours!

We had by now built up quite a reputation and my partner John and I found walking both dogs so stressful. In our house they were two beautifully-behaved dogs, but once the front door opened it got manic!

Several dog trainers, a German shepherd dog training school and hydrotherapy to try and get rid of her excess energy later, we finally discovered Ade!

He came to us for a visit and within **one afternoon** he had her sitting next to his dog Pip. I could have cried. I never thought I would see her calmly sitting outside, let alone next to another dog!

Since then we have worked at his training methods, attended some of his workshops whenever we need a bit of extra guidance and I can honestly say she is a totally different dog. She now desperately wants to meet other dogs and is slowly learning social skills from them. It is a joy to watch and a long way from where we started.

She still has her bad days where she can't cope, but I know her body language well enough to keep her away so she doesn't stress out! I never thought we would be in the park off-lead, throwing balls for them both and really enjoying the outdoors!

I now have an eight-month-old daughter whom all the dogs adore and she loves them! We have also welcomed another doggy member into our house, which I never thought we would be able to do. She and Tammy are the best of friends!

I cannot thank Ade enough for the knowledge and support he has given us over this journey!
Sarah Catton

A far happier Tammy

Tammy is the white dog in the middle, Pip on the left is doing his best to ignore her

Important note

I have been doing this a long time and with hundreds of dogs. You haven't. I can read the signs and know if a dog is going to bite or not. It's my job to make it change its mind and attitude.

Turning the Page

Page the Doberman bitch

We got our Doberman bitch called Page from a rescue centre when she was nearly five years old. She had already had three different homes and came with a list of problems, although these didn't seem to exist when she arrived.

She was a very well-behaved dog, with a good deal of training. She got on exceptionally well with our giant Schnauzer and was fine with the cats.

She would steal food if it was left out and could open all the kitchen cupboards and the doors in the house, but we could deal with these problems.

On walks, however, we discovered that occasionally if she met a dog that barked or growled at her she would attack them, grabbing them by the scruff of the neck and not letting go. She never drew blood. This happened on several occasions and we began to take her to places where we knew we wouldn't meet other dogs.

Training classes didn't help.

Pretty soon the problem began to ruin our lives. We couldn't take her anywhere and it was no pleasure owning her. Our other dog began to suffer because he didn't get to go anywhere to meet other dogs either.

With nothing to lose, we called Ade. When he arrived – within the week – he showed us how to control the doorway when greeting visitors, excellent for both dogs! (The General and Sentry technique.)

We had trouble lead walking so he took us out into the street, and showed us how to use the rope lead. We were amazed at the results: calm walking **within seconds**!

Then Page's arch enemy the Border Collie across the road came out and, as always, barked frantically at her. Ade showed us how to take control and demonstrate that we were the leaders and within minutes we were able to walk Page past the dog without Page batting an eyelid!

Now we know the techniques we have much more confidence that we can control Page – and she has confidence in us. It continues to be hard work but we can take her anywhere now; in fact we actively take her to busy dog places, so she can become better socialised.

She is a lot happier in her demeanour and less stressed when we leave her home alone.

Sarah Eley and Dave Walker

Another success story

Page and her owners have joined me several times on my pack walks and I have to say I was amazed at the difference in her. Sarah and Dave have done a remarkable job.

TO PERMANENTLY CHANGE A DOG'S BEHAVIOUR

YOU HAVE TO CHANGE THE OWNER'S BEHAVIOUR PERMANENTLY

SARAH AND DAVE CHANGED THE WAY THEY TREATED PAGE AND PAGE LOVED KNOWING WHAT THE RULES WERE AND TRUSTED HER NEW PACK LEADERS.

CHAPTER 5
Pulling on the lead

I have never met a dog that has wanted to walk behind me, but most dogs are happy to walk with their heads just in front of my legs so that they can see left and right as they walk along.

Most owners would be happy if their dogs did this instead of dragging them all over the place.

I see a lot of dogs that pull on the lead. A dog that pulls is very tiring and their owner ends up hating the walk. They may have suffered injuries such as pulled muscles, shoulder strains and back problems.

I get my clients to visualise a horse and jockey. The jockey is likely to weigh about 55 kilos. The horse might weigh 500 kilos or more. Yet the jockey is able to control the horse. How? The jockey controls the head of the horse using a bridle and bit. To slow the horse at the start of a race the jockey will rein in the horse by pulling back on the reins. The horse's head comes up and the horse slows down.

Control the head and you control the dog.

A lot of the head harness types of dog leads work on this principle; control the head and control the dog. I have never liked them for the simple reason that whenever I have put one on any dog, they will do their level best to remove it either with their paws or by scraping it along the ground.

I don't like the thought of my dog's head being trussed up like a beef joint and have met clients' dogs that have worn away all the fur below their eyes and others where the contraption has ridden up the face and is rubbing on the eye itself. There are kitchen drawers all over the country filled with numerous 'miracle' devices designed to stop a dog pulling.

The first thing to consider is simple mechanics.

A dog has to get its head down to pull. If you lift the head up the dog cannot use its weight to pull you.

Therefore you can stop the dog pulling by pulling the head up.

I use a gun dog slip lead with a rubber stopper in a choice of two lengths depending on the size of the dog and the height of the handler.

Place the lead high on the neck at the back of the jaw and up behind the ears

I place my thumb through the loop and lay the lead across my palm

Then I close my fingers over both ropes and this lets me hold my hand in a natural relaxed fist position but gives me complete control and the dog cannot easily pull the lead from my hand

Using a short leash (0.9m) for larger dogs

I am going to describe how to walk your dog on the **left-hand side** and describe it as a **male**. If you want to walk your dog on the right simply reverse the instructions.

1 Position the lead as high as you can on the neck, under the jaw and behind the ears. The tightness should feel the same as a man wearing a shirt with a buttoned collar: comfortable enough not to interfere with your breathing but not too loose.

2 Slide the toggle down to stop the lead loosening and keep it in place at the top of the neck.

3 Slip your left thumb through the handle loop and lay the lead across your open palm.

4 Then fold your fingers over the lead and grip the lead. The dog should be on the left.

Dogs usually walk at a trot. Hence the term **dog trot**. We are slower than a dog and consequently unless you jog along beside him, his natural speed will take him in front of you.

1 As he moves forward, allow your arm to extend forward, keeping the lead up and tug upwards if the dog moves too far forward. Do not pull back and down at waist height as many people do. You are simply getting into a pulling situation again and it will also pull the lead down its neck where it becomes ineffective.

2 Come to a slow stop. The dog's head will rise up and he will stop with very little pressure on the lead.

3 After a few turns and stops and walking back and forth, the dog will start to follow you, stopping when you stop and moving when you move. When you need to correct the dog use a short, snappy, double tug upwards and inwards towards your lower rib cage to stop yourself yanking the poor dog around.

4 To turn to the left you will need to position the dog's head beside your knee and start the turn with your left leg so that he can see your leg coming across his nose. I tuck the hand holding the lead into the small of my back. This shortens the lead and positions the dog next to my knee and because I keep my hand close to my body there is very little strain on my arm or shoulder. I position the dog and then start the left turn with my left leg. His head will move left and the body will follow. A few circles to the left will make the dog keep back as your leg is constantly across his nose.

5 Practise every day for 10 minutes. Left and right turns, figures of eight, slow and stop, change direction. You will have a different dog in a week.

Using a longer leash (1.5m) for smaller dogs

1 I hold the leash anchored in the right hand. I put my right hand through the loop and then grip the leash, using the left hand for correcting. The left arm can then remain relaxed. If the dog lunges forward and pulls the leash out of the left hand, you have it safely anchored with the right hand.

2 When turning left, I position the dog with my left hand on the leash and again start the turn with my left leg.

3 My right hand remains at my right side throughout. The leash falls across my thighs. With small dogs I may have to lift the leash with my left hand to avoid tripping over the leash.

4 I hold my right hand by my side and walk. I may help myself by tucking my thumb into my trouser pocket. The dog has to follow.

5 After a few minutes the dog realises that to avoid being dragged around by the neck he must pay attention to **me**, not everything else in the world.

6 I turn right, stop, walk, about turn, left turn, go around in a circle. The dog starts to follow and pay attention, looking up at me every few seconds. If the dog moves in front I do a right turn or an about turn and the dog is automatically positioned behind me.

7 Before it has a chance to move in front I may throw in a left turn and cut it off.

8 I may walk in left-hand circles for 20 or 30 seconds to get the dog to stay back. I say as little as possible as this is all about body language and building a rapport with your dog.

9 The dog will start to look up at you, instead of pulling and trying to get away. You can usually see a good result in less than 10 minutes.

10 You can then start to use a little vocal encouragement and see if the dog responds to that. Some do, some don't. This is another step in becoming a Pack Leader.

11 Walk at a good speed, as fast as you can manage to start with, then slow down and vary the pace. Stop, turn around and be in charge! Do not constantly look at the dog as you will automatically start to slow down. **Look straight ahead** most of the time, with a quick glance down occasionally to see where the dog is. The dog will understand you are walking with purpose and start to follow you.

12 If you can, walk as near to a dog trot as possible. This is more difficult with larger dogs for obvious reasons, but speed is one of the main factors in training.

A dog trot is their natural gait so help them out a bit. It's good for your heart too!

With certain dogs there may be protest behaviour such as pulling, trying to shake the collar off, digging the heels in, whining, spinning or jumping but the dog will finally realise that it has to walk beside the handler.

Put your right hand through loop and dog on the left side. This method is usually better for smaller dogs and the longer lead

A short lead gives you good control with a larger dog. Bringing the head up stops the dog using its weight against you

Tug corrections

If you hold the lead in your left hand, you can bend your arm upwards, give a couple of quick tugs upwards to make the dog check its stride and keep walking so that you catch up with the dog. I think it is better to do this than try the stop/wait/start method one sees in some training classes. The tug correction is a knack. It takes time to get right because it must be **applied with a slack lead**. If the lead is tight, you must draw the dog towards you slightly to create a bit of slack and then use the snap tug, that's why I use the double tug. The first tug gives you a bit of slack the second tug corrects the dog.

Common owner errors

- Incorrect length of leash for dog size
- Walking too slowly
- Starting at a good speed but then slowing down
- Stopping to allow the dog to pee or scent a lot
- Correcting too often so that the correction becomes meaningless
- Staring down at the dog all the time
- Winding up the leash; it restricts the dog's movement and winds up the dog
- Turning a tug-and-release correction into a tug-and-pull-and-strangle-the-dog!
- Correcting as you turn. Just turn, hold the leash by your side, and let the dog follow. Don't yank.

A dog can be choked by any collar. If you position the leash correctly, not tight but not loose and high up on the neck behind the ears, and then apply the correct technique, the result is almost miraculous.

Like a lot of things, it is easy when you know how.

How much money do people waste on collars and harnesses thinking it will solve the problem?

CASE
HISTORY

Pulling on the lead.

**Here's Valentino,
70 kg of Newfoundland.**

His owner Monica weighed 21 kilos less than Valentino and attempted to walk him with a head harness, an ordinary collar and lead and a body harness all at the same time to try to control him.

Valentino took Monica for a walk, not the other way around!

If he didn't want to go home Valentino would simply lie down on the park and wouldn't budge.

I showed how to use the slip lead effectively and had Valentino walking without pulling very quickly.

There was a little protest from Valentino when he realised we were in control but we were quite gentle on him and cajoled him into following the lead rather than making him hate it. We tried to interact more with him as we walked so that his attention wasn't totally on the scents drifting along from every lamppost. We kept up a good pace to get him to follow us rather than allow him to drag us along and made ourselves more interesting by playing with him on the park.

In my opinion a lot of dog owners do not interact with their dogs enough on a walk. They meet people in the park and spend most of the walk chatting with them instead of actually playing with and enjoying their dog. No wonder their dogs don't pay them any attention!

CHAPTER 6
Jumping up

Why do dogs jump up? There are several reasons which I have learned from observing dogs interacting with each other and with humans.

Dogs like to greet face to face. They want eye contact. They want to smell what you have had for lunch and lick your face.

As you are on your hind legs they may jump up to look you in the eye. Try getting down to their level to see if they jump up, but watch out for bony heads and sharp claws. Whenever I crouch down to greet my dogs I have to be careful I don't get a whack on the face from Buster, my Airedale, who loves to throw his head around and rub his body against me to say hello.

Dogs like to be fussed, so they will come up to you in an excited state, tail wagging. They may try to get attention with rear-end wagging, pawing or by jumping up. If you fuss them every time they come up to you with this request, they have trained you to fuss them on demand. Give fuss when you decide, not them.

Dogs do not know that their behaviour is unacceptable to humans until we tell them.

By telling them in a dog way you will get instant results. If you try to do it in a human way you could be there for ever.

How to stop a dog jumping up

1 The knee bump
Use a straight knee bump to move the dog away or overbalance it. Verbally correct with a low, short and sharp "NO" and stare at the dog. This usually works very quickly, within minutes if you get it right. The dog realises it is not getting any fuss or attention and is also getting corrected. A double whammy!

When you use the knee bump, keep your foot on the floor and raise your heel which will bring the knee up sharply into the dog's chest. It is only a bump – you are not trying to hurt the dog or propel it over the garden fence, so be sensible. The bump is far more important than the "NO", by the way. I tell people to keep their foot on the floor so that no-one thinks you are kicking or being cruel to the dog. However if a very large dog jumps on me, I will lift my knee up sharply to protect myself. I don't feel the need to add to the numerous scars and bite marks I have received over the years!

I am also indicating to the dog that I am not its friend, playmate or equal but a higher rank so it should respect my personal space and not jump all over me like a new best friend.

2 Trapping paws
Dogs hate being trapped, so trapping its paws will make a dog want to get away from you and reluctant to repeat the chance of getting trapped.

With larger dogs it is easy to grab their front paws when they jump up. With smaller ones you can sit down. Wear gloves if you don't fancy being mouthed while you have hold of their paws.

It is important not to look at the dog when you are holding its paws, eye contact is one of the things it wants. When it tries to get away hold on until it is really pulling away and then release the paws with a verbal "NO" and a knee bump for good measure.

Now step away and call the dog to you. If it comes with all four feet on the floor you can give it a stroke on the head and a "good boy" if you feel so inclined. Don't overdo the praise*. Soon the dog will learn that jumping up results in getting trapped.

3 Blocking
In the park, you can use your hand, a ball launcher or a walking stick to block the area in front of you and claim your personal space with other people's dogs.

Or do as I do and put them on their backside with a firm knee bump – the dog never bothers me again.

4 Turning away/ignoring
Most trainers use this method. I don't.

Plenty of my clients agree with me that it does not work.

Dogs are not telepathic. If you simply turn away from the dog how will it know it has done wrong? I prefer to tell the dog it has done wrong in a way it quickly understands.

Methods one and two in my experience are much better than the others – they will always work.

I find a combination of trapping paws followed by a gentle knee bump usually works in minutes and is permanent.

Case history

I went to see a couple with an eight-month-old Gordon Setter. Freddie was a gorgeous-looking dog but he kept jumping up at the husband, whose arms were covered in scratches and bruises: the Setter could almost reach his shoulders with his paws. I asked his wife if the dog jumped up her at all.

'Well he did to start with,' she said, 'but then I got fed up and threw him off me and he landed on his backside and never jumped up again.'

I explained that in dog language she had told the dog 'I am not your friend, I am not your playmate, I am a senior rank and I demand you respect my personal space.' The dog understood straight away.

*Praise is an overworked tool

Used by trainers when often no praise is necessary. If you told your child to sit at the table and read a book you wouldn't immediately run over to him, fuss him and give him a biscuit, would you? So why do it to a dog?

One current training trend is to 'ignore the bad behaviour and reward the good'.

In my opinion there is absolutely no logic to this method.

Anyone with an ounce of sense can see it is absurd. Keep well clear of trainers who use this method.

CLEAR SIGNALS PLEASE

A man says to his wife "Why are you ignoring me? Have I done something wrong?"

"Well if you don't know, I'm not going to tell you" replies his wife.

"Well I don't know, that's why I'm asking" says the man.

Men and dogs. We are simple creatures. So make it clear. Don't hint, don't suggest, just make it clear.

PLAIN ENGLISH FOR MEN.
CLEAR SIGNALS FOR DOGS.

CHAPTER 7
Aggression lesson

How a severe bite taught me a lesson in dog training.

I was contacted by Jason who lived in Middlesex. He had a young English Mastiff called Max. Max was 12 months old and weighed a solid nine stone. He had been to training classes and had previously been a well-behaved and much-loved pet.

To cut a long story short, he had bitten two people in the previous two weeks and was under sentence of death if I could not fix him. I arranged to see Max the following week. Jason was there to meet me, with Ruth his wife, who had helped to raise Max from a puppy. Max had not bitten anyone before, except in play, and that could better be described as mouthing rather than biting. However, as he was now getting rather big, this behaviour was unacceptable.

As renovation work was being carried out on their house, Jason, Ruth and Max were temporarily staying at Jason's parents' home where a five year old Chihuahua thought it was the boss of the house.

When I arrived the Chihuahua barked at me and growled and kept making little mock charges.

Max was in the back garden and there was a barrier between the conservatory door and the garden to keep him out of the house. No-one could fathom out why he had suddenly turned on people. I took one look at Max from inside the conservatory and asked Jason to put a lead on him as he was fixated on me and was standing still and staring.

These were the warning signs. As soon as I got outside and approached Max from behind to avoid eye contact, he lunged for me, went low and bit my ankle.

Fortunately I am aware of a dog's favourite targets and always wear ankle boots for protection. I got Jason to put the slip lead high on Max's neck so that I could get some control over his head and this led to 10 to 15 minutes of protest by Max. He was rolling around on the floor, biting the lead, putting his paws over the lead and trying to pull away and finally he jumped up and bit me on the arm to try to make me release him. I held on and used the knee bump to make him back off.

I showed how to control and correct with the slip lead using a snap tug and release but Max was quite wound up by this time and when I went behind him he leapt up from a lying position and jumped up towards my face. I managed to turn my face away, but his snapping jaws connected with my chest just to the right of my nipple and sank his teeth into my flesh. He released me instantly, and Jason managed to pull him away. I had a full set of Mastiff teeth marks and blood started to ooze out and stain my shirt. One of his incisors had penetrated the skin and made a bit of a hole but fortunately I am quite skinny and there wasn't a lot of flesh to get hold of. Max sat next to Jason and stared at me.

I decided to try barging in order to change the way Max regarded me. I asked Jason to nudge Max on the shoulder to distract him and make him look away from me. Max ignored the first nudge and stared at me. He was planning his next attack. I told Jason that the barge must be strong enough to make the dog look away and realise its behaviour is unacceptable. Jason drew back his knee and gave Max a resounding thump in his ribs. I don't think Jason intended to be quite so firm, and it certainly took me by surprise, but the change in Max was immediate. He stopped looking at me and when I asked Jason to walk around me Max tried to move away from me instead of staring and weighing up the chances of getting close enough to attack. I asked Jason to stop about two metres from me. Max sat next to him without being asked but the most amazing thing was he sat down facing **AWAY** from me. He would not even look at me anymore. His owner had told him in a way he understood that his behaviour was unacceptable, so he had chosen to go into avoidance. I was in his personal space and because he knew he could not be aggressive or run away, his only other choice was avoidance, so he sat down in a submissive position and faced away from me to avoid direct eye contact.

I continued to do some exercises with Jason and Ruth to stop Max trying to chase the chickens in the pen and some lead control exercises as well. Ruth was able to walk Max around the chicken run in complete control for the first time ever.

After a break for lunch there was a knock at the front door and a delivery man started to bring in a number of boxes containing parts of a wardrobe.

The Chihuahua barked aggressively and attached itself to his boot and a light went off in my head.

I realised that the five-year-old Chihuahua thought its job was to attack any stranger that came into the house. Max the nine-stone Mastiff had learned from the Chihuahua and started to bite people as well. Young dogs learn from older dogs. So if the older dog is misbehaving, the likelihood is that the younger dog will copy the behaviour.

Small breeds such as Chihuahuas, Westies and other small terriers are allowed to become quite aggressive to humans and other dogs because humans are too soft with them. **"Oh he's so cute, he's good in the house and I love him to bits. He just doesn't like visitors, blah, blah, blah."**

Wake up and smell the coffee, your dog is in charge of the house and thus aggressive. If it were a large breed, you would sort it out promptly before a visit from the local constabulary, but because the dog is a cute little pooch it is allowed to attack people. So it is kept behind a door and barks continuously – sometimes until the visitor has left.

The experience taught me several things.
Young dogs learn from older dogs no matter what the size.
The Mastiff had learned from the older Chihuahua.

A barge with the knee can be very powerful, and can change
a dog's behaviour in seconds.

Never wear a new shirt to see an aggressive dog.

Carry a first aid kit.

The scar has faded now but the image of Max's snapping teeth
inches from my face is seared into my memory.

Barging

I first used a barge or a nudge with my knee some years ago
as a distraction tool to stop a dog staring at another dog and pay
attention to me.

I had noticed that dogs when playing would lean against other dogs
as they ran beside each other. Some dogs would jump on the backs
of others as a test of strength or dominance or both. They appeared
to use this type of play to sort out the pecking order in the pack.

A few dogs would adopt a very upright posture with their tail up
and their head over the shoulder of another dog as a sign of
dominance. The other dog might submit and show submissive
signs or square up and a confrontation might occur, usually just
a growl and an air snap.

None of my dogs will allow another dog to do this without turning
and growling or snapping at the other dog. It is bad manners
to put the head over the shoulder of another; it can be interpreted
as bullying. I found that by using my knee on the back of the neck
to barge a dog I was simulating what a senior dog would do
and I could immediately get a dog to go into a submissive pose.
I have found it to be a very powerful and successful tool when
dealing with dogs that are aggressive to people.

One client arrived at my home with a large German Shepherd
in the back of her car. It was three years old and it had never been
off-lead with other dogs because it lunged and snapped. It would
also try to attack visitors to the house, so it had become very
isolated and so had its owner.

He was taught
to bite visitors
by a Chihuahua

This jumping is part
of their play not
aggression

Dog play can seem
quite aggressive
but there are rules
to avoid fights

I approached the car where the dog was barking and snarling in the back, showing all its teeth. The owner asked me if I wanted her to get the dog out of the car. I wasn't wild about the idea but I said to go ahead.

She put the dog on a lead and brought it out. It was barking and lunging towards me in a very aggressive manner. I have to admit I was expecting to get a bite. It was a scary moment.

I grasped the lead at arm's length and immediately gave a quick, sharp tug to distract the dog from jumping up for a second. As all four feet touched the floor, I brought my knee firmly down on the back of its neck.

The dog immediately sat down and looked at me. I stared at it and it looked away. I turned to walk away, the dog followed the lead, and I walked it up and down the road to heel.
I approached the owner and tugged the lead and the dog sat down and looked at me. To be honest we were all quite shocked. The owner, the dog and me!

I was astonished at how quickly the dog had submitted and shown me respect. I had said to the dog: 'Is that all you've got? Take this barge and if you want some more and think you are hard enough, come and have a go!'

I never uttered a word throughout.

Within two hours the dog was off-lead in my back garden with Pip and Buster. The first time it had ever been with other dogs in **three years**.

After that I started experimenting with barging dogs on the neck, shoulders and sides.

I had remarkable results for various aggressive behaviours. I would never refuse to see a dog no matter how aggressive it appeared and I accepted the occasional bite as a part of the job, so I got plenty of experience as word spread that I could actually change a dog's behaviour really quickly. People would talk about this mad man who would front up even the most aggressive dog. I found I could read a dog in minutes and developed a method using a series of carefully-controlled exercises to confront and correct a dog in a way it understood.

I found that most of the dogs were bluffing; their behaviour was mostly bravado, and they did not want a full-on fight. They were usually nervous and unsure of what to do, so their self-defence instinct kicked in. Instead of choosing avoidance, they chose nervous aggression.

Once I had confronted the aggression and the dog had shown me submission I would then start to build a relationship as the dog's leader.

I always ask the owner to put a lead on the dog. If I go near the dog's head with my hands and
a lead, it is a good way to get bitten. I am presenting the dog with an easy target, so the owner puts the lead on and hands it to me.

The dog will now want to get away from me. Its aggressiveness has not worked. This big animal on two legs (that's me!) has not backed down, so a dog's natural reaction is to run away.

Because I have the dog on a lead it cannot run away so it has only one option left. It has to show me submissive behaviour.

I simply stand and hold the lead, ignoring the dog. If it tries to walk or crawl away I pull it back beside me. It usually lies down on the floor or sits and faces away from me to avoid eye contact. It is displaying visual signals to indicate submission and avoidance. Any growl is immediately corrected with a snap tug of the lead and a sharp **"A"** bark. I immediately release any tension on the lead and ignore the dog again.

I want the dog to realise that as long as it shows me respect and submission it is quite safe. I stop using the visual and vocal threat signals and it starts to relax.

Next, I take the dog for a walk, making sure I am in charge. In dog language, I am asking it to join my pack and follow me. I put in plenty of left and right turns, changing speed, and I stop and start occasionally. I use an encouraging high-toned voice as I move off and the dog's body language changes within minutes. I teach the owner these skills so that they can deal with any situation.

If a dog is aggressive with dogs as well as humans I carry out a series of confrontation and avoidance exercises with my own dogs before allowing it to mix freely with them in the garden.

Experience has taught me when the time is right.

Barging has proved to be a powerful tool in correcting a wayward dog without causing it any harm or making it fearful. On the contrary, clear direction and leadership help to calm the dog; it learns to respect humans and start to behave like a normal dog again.

CASE HISTORY

Aggressive Bulldog

Bomber the English Bulldog
by Wendy Shipp

I contacted Ade with a problem I had with my English Bulldog Bomber aged four and a half.

I'd had him from eight weeks old and he was a loving companion until about 12 months ago.

By then, however, he had become extremely aggressive towards me and other people when he didn't get his own way. He had bitten me a few times, sending me A&E a couple of times. He had jumped up at other people and I was extremely concerned that he would do some serious harm.

We went to several dog training classes and he managed to get his Silver award in the Kennel Club Scheme. I just couldn't understand why he was behaving in such a way; I had never mistreated him, always ensured that fresh water was available, fed him with quality food, taken him out for walks, played with him to ensure he wasn't bored… But he kept on (almost) biting the hand that fed him.

I really couldn't take much more. I had been to two other trainers for advice and tried their techniques to no avail. I had had sleepless nights worrying about what would happen next. Had the time come for me to have him destroyed? The thought sickened me and brought me to tears time after time. I loved this dog.

The internet was my next hope and I searched desperately for someone to help. There they were: several reviews on Ade Howe. I contacted him straight away and he made an appointment to visit the house and see for himself what was happening. He came to the door and I knew what was going to happen. Bomber, who is 34 kg, charged at the door and started to attack Ade, biting his feet, jumping up at him and growling. I was horrified and wondered what on earth Ade could do to help.

Within a few minutes Ade had put Bomber in his place, after the dog had made several attempts to bite and attack him. I couldn't believe my eyes. This man had entered my house and within 10 minutes had Bomber acknowledging him and doing as he was told. Ade showed me how to address the situation, how to control the space and show Bomber who was in command.

Next, we went outside into the street and Ade showed me what was required. We continued by going into my place of work where Bomber comes in the afternoon and again I was given clear and concise instructions as to what was required.

BOMBER

Here's Bomber, 34 kilos
of English Bulldog

A month of following Ade's instructions, being firm and showing Bomber that I am the pack leader has worked wonders. Bomber is now relaxed and enjoying life and not being on guard 24/7.

I am able to let people into the house, although he is still a little wary with strangers. I'm sure that is to be expected, especially when he doesn't know them. I am also able to pull him off the sofa and push him outside whenever I want and believe me I was never able to do such a thing before Ade came along.

I have my beautiful Bulldog back. He has given me so much pleasure and joy and we have a lovely life together. I still have to be extremely firm and never let him get the better of me, and ensure that he knows I am the pack leader at all times. I cannot thank Ade enough. He has given me back my dog and writing this short story brings tears of joy to my eyes.

Thank you Ade, with all my heart.
Wendy

CASE HISTORY

George Bush

George Bush the German shepherd
George Bush; he was named because we spent four or five hours one very wet October Sunday trying to encourage him out of a bush, together with a couple of friends from the village and two police officers. George just wanted to growl and showed his teeth. He was very scared, thin and hungry. After he ran loose through our village, I managed to corner him in a fenced field and called for back up.

We think he was 12 months old then and he's coming up to 22 months old now.

We already had a black and white Border collie, Tipsy, also a rescue at around 18 weeks. She's seven now. The hardest part of the journey to date has been getting the two of them together. This has only happened in the past eight weeks! It's taken 10 months.

George showed nervous aggression. He clearly had an awful start to life and a male has been very mean to him. He eventually came out of the bushes for water and snacks and the growls and teeth disappeared. No dog warden was available at the weekend so the Police encouraged us to take him overnight if we could. He was already my dog by then.

He spent 14 days as a guest of the council at a wonderful rescue centre, Ardley Rescue Centre in Bicester. Anabel took care of him, although as he was such a whinger and clearly very scared she renamed him Georgina! (He's a bit of a sissy, all bark and no bite.)

So home he came, much to the disgust of Tipsy! She did not want to accept him and very soon George had decided that this was 'his house'. We used a crate in the early days, a place of safety for him, and he still sleeps in it. We had weeks and weeks of dog segregation, sleepless nights and stress. Had we done the right thing? Could we cope with this?

Eventually we found Ade. He came over and spent a few hours with us showing us how to establish a higher rank than George. George had taken control of us, our home and our lives!

Gary became the boss within days of Ade's visit. Ade showed us simple, clear techniques to assert our ranking and be the leader over both of them. I found this harder, and still do. I give George the sympathy vote too much, which I know from reading lots about it, is the worst thing I can do. I am getting better at this.

George has a few friends who are allowed to play with him and a few others he isn't ready to accept. We socialise him every day and people who know us in our village are aware of what we are trying to do, so they accept that he may bark sometimes! Chasing cars when on a lead walk is ongoing with both dogs, the slip lead helps and the knee bump and "A" help.

GEORGE BUSH

Ade was a turning point in our rehabilitation of George. Without him, I dread to think. We were having a real rocky patch with him at that time. Confidence, dominance and a few simple techniques and look where we are now!
Clare, Gary, Meg, George and Tipsy

CHAPTER 8
Nuisance barking

What is nuisance barking?

It is barking which is inappropriate or unexplained and persistent.

There are lots of different reasons for it.

A puppy may constantly bark at their owner to get attention or to initiate play. This is **request barking** and can sometimes carry on for hours.

I have successfully developed several successful methods to stop this. Block the dog into a corner with your legs. It will stop barking. If it is jumping up as well, use the knee bump. Or try the same method as dogs that don't want to play: stick your chin in the air and move your head away from the dog (See Chapter **I'm not interested**).

One of these methods usually gets results – in minutes.

A puppy may bark to greet other dogs or react to humans who are giving certain visual and vocal signals.
I worked with a six-month-month old Cairn Terrier, which barked constantly in the vet's waiting room. His bark was so loud and high-pitched it drowned out people on the telephone and he had to be taken outside. I worked with him and the owners at their home first and then visited the vet's premises.

The dog did not bark for several minutes until the receptionist said in a high-pitched voice "oh Freddie, aren't you a good boy? You're doing so well". Freddie immediately started barking at her. It's not always the dog's fault…

Guarding: a dog may bark at the slightest sound or movement inside or outside the dwelling.
The dog will give a warning bark or woof even though the owner may not have heard anything.

This behaviour is very common and can cause a lot of other problems, because the dog has become stressed. The solution is to define the dog's job and communicate with it so that it knows when to react to noises and when to ignore them. The owner must **take control** of the house and relieve the dog of the stress of being on Sentry duty all the time. Use the General and Sentry method and correct each time the dog overreacts to noises (Chapter 3).

Barking when let out into the garden.
The dog is let into the garden and just barks for no apparent reason and will not stop.

Another symptom of stress and over-guarding…

I think the dog gets stressed out and needs to have a release of some kind. It barks to vent its frustration. When the owner starts shouting "shut up" the dog thinks they are joining in and views it as approval.

I usually start with **taking control** in the house and often this is enough to cure the problem outside. I then take control of the garden by getting between the fence and the dog and moving the dog away from the fence.

If this doesn't work I may use **an action/ consequence technique**. Negative behaviour can be changed a lot quicker when the dog associates it with a negative consequence. A garden hose can be useful for this. Barking at the fence gets a squirt with the hose to surprise, distract and correct the dog. The dog soon learns not to bark because it doesn't like getting wet. This technique doesn't work with every dog (some dogs just love the hose!) but I have found it extremely effective in most instances.

Barking through the front window of the house, at passers by and visitors. It is quite common for people to allow their dogs to sit on top of a chair at their front window and bark at everything and everyone passing by. This is not normal dog behaviour – take a minute to think about it.

In the wild, a pack of dogs will observe all the animals that pass as a potential meal, or perhaps a predator. In either case barking would not be a good idea! That lunch, alerted to their presence, would disappear pretty fast, and a predator would think "ah ha, there's the dinner bell" and head straight for the dogs.

The natural reaction in the wild is to keep quiet and observe.

A house dog is, of course, in a different situation, especially if it doesn't have other dogs to learn from. It tries to work out for itself what to do. Not all dogs that sit on the back of a chair will bark at people passing. Some just watch. It is the barkers that you need to sort out.

The house dog will see someone it thinks is approaching the house and bark a warning. The person may be just on their way to the shops for a pint of milk and a paper, but the dog thinks it has chased it away and done its duty. Its owner has either ignored its behaviour or joined in with the barking ("stop it, Freddie!") so it must be doing a good job.

I would move the chair so that the dog cannot stand guard on it. Use the General and Sentry method to take control of the window. Get a neighbour or friend to walk by several times with a selection of coats and hats and correct the dog **each time** it starts to bark. It has to learn that its job is to bark at the door only and to stop when told.

Usually the dog will stop this behaviour within 10 minutes or so.

A dog may bark when left alone in the house. This could be **boredom** or **separation anxiety**.

A dog that is fed, watered and well-exercised will happily sleep for several hours, but owners should try to avoid leaving a dog for more than a few hours. A working day of eight hours plus travel might mean your dog is alone in the house for 10 hours or more. This is not a good idea, and if you think you have to be away from the house for this length of time each working day, it might be an idea to reconsider dog owning. A dog needs a life and company, and if it has your attention for only two or three hours in every 24, it will get lonely and bored. Bored dogs will find ways to amuse themselves, just like children. They could try to dig or chew their way out of your house, causing a lot of expensive damage.

A dog may barking at people and dogs when out on the lead.
This is usually because the dog is nervous and barking to make people or other dogs keep away. This can develop into mock attacks: barking, rushing forward and then retreating, especially if it is a small dog.

The solution is to **take control in the house** so that you become the dog's pack leader, then take control of the lead and the walk. Correct any barking with the lead tug, vocal correction and a nudge if necessary and you will find the dog starts to follow your lead and remain calm. It may even start to hide behind you if it is really nervous. Show it that you are the pack leader, and give the dog some confidence that you are in charge and will protect it. It will follow you, with relief.

CHAPTER 9
Mouthing

Mouthing is when a dog keeps putting its teeth on you.

It may be very gentle or it may draw blood.

Puppies do a lot of mouthing because they are like human babies in that respect: everything goes in the mouth for testing. Babies grow out of it but some dogs will mouth for years if they are not taught to stop. Mouthing is a common and normal behaviour in puppies.

When puppies are growing up with other puppies they learn to inhibit their bite so that they don't damage each other. If a puppy bites too hard, the other puppy will yelp and may then growl, snarl and snap back. Usually this results in play stopping immediately.

Puppies do not usually mouth senior ranked dogs. I took my dogs to see a couple of young puppies that were playing non-stop rough and tumble. As soon as my three dogs walked in the play stopped and the puppies never attempted to mouth my dogs so they must have somehow signalled to the puppies that they weren't interested. However both puppies mouthed the owners and one had nipped the man when he had tried to stop one of them digging the lawn.

There were also problems with general grooming and wiping the eyes as the little Labradoodle would turn and bite and wriggle around.

I blocked it into a corner and used the General and Sentry method to get it to sit and stay in two minutes. This immediately ranked me above the dog. I also used a quick finger poke on the flank to simulate a corrective nip from a senior dog. When it came to the grooming problem I picked up the dog, put it on my knee and just started brushing it and talked to it in a gentle voice. It just sat there and looked at me quite happily. I then handed it over to the owner who took a wet cotton pad and wiped its eyes with no protest at all.

This demonstrates that it regarded me as a higher rank and not a playmate so it did not mouth me. The whole process took about 10 minutes.

On another occasion I was contacted by a very upset lady experiencing horrendous play-biting from Millie her 4 month old Cockerpoo.

When I arrived at the house the following week, Millie's owner showed me her arms which were covered in bite marks, bruises and scratches from Millie's play-biting. A swift mock charge, finger poke to the flank and a verbal correction stopped her biting both owners within 20 minutes of my arrival.

Be careful of the little nippers

This young pup left a fine set of teeth marks on my finger when I went to cure his nipping

I advise owners to try to direct biting and chewing to the things you don't mind them chewing such as a tug rope, a rawhide chew or similar.

Millie didn't like being groomed at all as her coat easily got matted and it hurt to tug a brush through it.

I gave her a hide chew to focus her teeth on and gently brushed her in one small area before moving on to the next. Grooming should be a pleasant experience for both dog and owner. Groom slowly and try not to tug the brush through a matted coat. It may be easier to cut the matted bit out or gently tease it apart.

I never praise a dog for not chewing me. There is no logic to introducing positive reinforcement here. I tell them off in a way they understand and then carry on as normal.

It's simple and effective.

URBAN MYTH

GET PEOPLE TO FEED YOUR DOG TO MAKE FRIENDS.

Dogs that start guarding the home to the point where they start to nip people or get aggressive are a common problem.

Do not think your dog is unique if it starts to do this.

If a trainer suggests the following method to cure it you should walk away as it is very dangerous.

Lock your dog in a room away from the front door and let your visitors in and allow them to make themselves comfortable. Then let the dog in and get your visitors to throw them titbits or feed them so that the dog starts to associate visitors with something good – more food.

YOU SHOULD NEVER EVER EVER DO THIS.

IT IS EXTREMELY DANGEROUS AND I KNOW OF PEOPLE THAT HAVE BEEN BADLY BITTEN USING THIS STUPID METHOD.

If the dog is guarding to the point of starting to show aggression or even biting, the owner is not in control.

In fact, the owner is having to change the way they live to accommodate the bad behaviour of the dog.

If the visitors are seated when the dog comes into the room the dog is almost at eye level. This makes it much more likely that the dog will challenge a human. I NEVER sit down in a client's home until I know the dog is safe to be with.

If your dog is wound up and your visitors are scared of it, you are just asking for trouble by offering food.

Your visitor's hand could become an easy target to bite. This is just crazy.

This is not a corrective technique it is using food to distract a dog.

You need to claim the house back, establish that ALL humans are a higher rank and use the General and Sentry method to gain control.

CHAPTER 10
I'm not interested

How to tell your dog play time is over.

Some clients have a problem with young dogs constantly asking them to play especially in the evenings when they want to settle down and watch TV. Maybe the dog has been on its own during the day while the owner has been at work or busy keeping the house clean and tidy or working from home.

In a few cases the dog may nag the owner for a couple of hours, barking constantly. Nothing seems to work and the owner is driven mad by a high pitched bark demanding: "play with me, play with me, play with me".

Some dogs will constantly seek attention from people, continually licking or nuzzling them.

It is a form of control. I often say to clients your dog has got you well-trained to give affection on demand!

It had me puzzled for quite a while, until I decided to let my dogs show me the solution.

Pip didn't play with other dogs. He loved his ball and me. He did not like people fussing him and he did not want to join in the play on the park with younger dogs.

Buster the Airedale is known as Mr Cool because he trots around the park well away from the rest of the dogs at a distance of up to 40 metres or more. He will meet and greet the other dogs, but mostly he does his own thing.

I studied Pip and Buster when young puppies or adolescent dogs ran up to them and tried to get them to play.

They put their chins high up in the air and moved their heads away. If the dog moved to the other side they moved their head away again. Within seconds, it seemed that the younger dogs knew this visual signal meant "I'm not interested so get lost".

I decided to try it out on Jack, my young Cocker Spaniel. Later that evening I sat on the floor and Jack immediately came over for a fuss and put his paws on my shoulders to get next to my face. After a bit of fuss and grooming I sat up straight, put my chin in the air and moved my head away from him. Within seconds he just moved away and lay down on the other side of the room.

I was gobsmacked. So simple, so clever, yet so effective. I'd never seen it in any dog training manual, book or video.

It was a revelation to me and another confirmation that dogs communicate mostly with visual signals.

Since then I've used it with many attention-seeking dogs with remarkable results. Clients may be sceptical at first, but when they see the results, they soon change their minds!

Try it. It works.

CHAPTER 11
Positions of power

In many homes the resident dog is unsure of its ranking in the pack.

It may try to control its environment and the people who enter or try to leave the home.

A dog prefers to challenge eye to eye. It may use your furniture to get to your eye level. Positions of power are sofas and chairs, beds, halfway up the stairs just above your eye level and at the top of the stairs from where they can look down on you.

Small dogs may also hide under a coffee table or behind a sofa and refuse to come out, trying to force you to get down to their level and when you reach out for their collar your hand becomes an easy target.

If you are sitting on the sofa and your dog is next to you it can more easily challenge at eye level. I have experience of dogs that would sit on their owner's shoulders or lie on the back of the sofa with a paw on top of the owner's head. Sometimes the owner would report that the dog would growl at them if they tried to move the dog off the sofa. It wasn't a surprise to me that the dogs were having leadership issues.

I have seen dogs that won't let their owners on the bed and refuse to get off it without a fight. The owners' bed is the highest and best nesting site in the house so access and control of it may allow your pet to think it is top dog.

One Staffordshire bull terrier I was working with ran away from me during training and disappeared up the stairs. **"I think he may have met his match"** said the owner but I thought he had given up too early. Sure enough, as I walked down the hall his face appeared through the banisters just above my eye level.

Dogs can be quite crafty.

On a visit to another house I entered the living room to find a large German shepherd with his paws on the arm of the sofa, barking right in my face.

The worst situations are when the dog has no respect for humans at all and has already bitten most if not all of the household. It gets to the stage where the dog attacks any stranger that enters the house. These are the scariest dogs I have to deal with as they will just launch an attack without warning. I have had a few moments when I thought I was going to get really mauled but have been lucky to escape with just a flesh wound. Thankfully these cases are relatively isolated but demonstrate that unless the owner takes the right corrective measures things can end in tragedy.

Dogs will use your furniture to bring them up to eye level with you

Tess retreated to a position of power just above my eye line

Beauty was aggressive with his family members after some traumatic incidents and tried to stop people leaving the room by nipping at their ankles. He had also attacked every member of the family at some point

My advice is:

- Not to allow your dogs on the bed or in the bedroom.
- Keep your dog off the furniture by claiming it as your own.
- Don't allow your dog to lie at the top of the stairs or halfway down.
- Use a broom instead of your hand to move a dog from underneath a coffee table. If it tries to bite the broom there is no harm done.
- Claim your dog's bed by standing or kneeling in it. You'd be surprised how many dogs seem taken aback to find me in the space they thought was under their control.

Small dogs may defend their bed/cage

Foxie the Pomeranian felt threatened by almost any visitor. Here he is defending the small opening of his cage as it is protected on all other sides. To challenge him you would have to get down to his eye level and then give him a target such as a hand which he can then bite to keep you away. Note the stare, mouth closed, ears back ready to snap.

URBAN MYTH

GOING THROUGH A DOOR FIRST MAKES YOU A DOG'S PACK LEADER.

RUBBISH!

The fact is you can go through a door in front of your dog a thousand times, but it won't make you a pack leader.

Most people I meet control their dogs by opening and closing doors or stair gates and putting the dog on a lead.

If you cannot control your dog in your own house what difference does it make if you go through a door first. It is complete rubbish. There is no logic to it.

You should be able to open your front door and keep your dog inside without it running off down the street.

You should be able to keep your dog out of the kitchen without closing the door.

You should be able to teach your dog that upstairs is out of bounds to dogs without having to use a stair gate.

These are the things that make you a pack leader.

CHAPTER 12
Separation
anxiety

Dogs often become very attached to people and when left on their own may display different kinds of difficult behaviour because they are separated from their owner. This is relatively easy and quick to fix if you use the correct methods and understand why the dog is stressed.

Here is a list of behaviour I have encountered during the past few years:

- Barking, howling or whining for hours on end
- Trying to dig through, around or under a door or gate. I have been to homes with shredded carpets, holes in the plasterboard by a door, floor coverings ripped up, the door frame destroyed. One dog even ripped off the architrave surrounding the door. I have been in kitchens where every single cupboard door had teeth marks on it and there were also teeth marks on the steel fridge door
- Constant jumping up at a door
- Licking the door frame or a window
- Messing in the house when the owners were out and then jumping all over the furniture and spreading it everywhere

- Self-harm such as gnawing or licking fur until the skin is bare and bleeding
- Ripped toes and nose damage from breaking out of a metal crate
- Damaged curtains or destroyed blinds
- Excessive panting and water consumption
- Tail chasing and biting
- One dog emptied all the floor level kitchen cupboards and managed to smash all the crockery.

Animals are tough on their offspring. They look after them completely for a while, and when they judge they are ready, they push them away to make them learn to feed themselves and become independent. It is in the interest of the herd that every member grows up quickly and keeps the herd strong. The weakest and dependent will not survive.

A sheep, for instance, will suckle its lamb for a time, but then it will decide it is time for the lamb to become independent and start to eat grass. The lamb wants the easy option: full fat milk on tap. The mother will drive the lamb away; she may kick out or butt the lamb quite hard in order to stop it trying to suckle and start grazing as soon as possible.

I have seen footage of a deer kicking out at its fawn to get it to start grazing and become independent.

Dog puppies born in the wild are suckled by their mother, but eventually she will need to hunt to restore her strength and produce more milk. She will usually leave the pups in the care of a den mother and go and hunt with the pack.

Hopefully they will kill and eat something and she will return to the den, produce more milk and suckle the pups. The older puppies that have been weaned but are not old enough to hunt will lick around the mouth of the returning adult dogs to try to get them to regurgitate some meat for them to eat. In this way the puppies learn to be independent but have the security of siblings and other members of the pack.

With the domestic dog however, the situation is very different.

The pup is removed from its mother and siblings within 12 weeks, sometimes as little as eight, and placed in a weird world of locked doors and windows, noisy machinery, loud noises and traffic. The dog has to try to make sense of this.

A fragile animal may become attached to the human they identify as their mother and follow them everywhere. This can go on for years. I have treated a Shi Tzu aged 10 for separation anxiety. Whenever it was left alone, it sat by the front door drooling so much that the wooden floor was stained. It scratched at the door to get out. It scratched itself a lot as it was wearing a jumper when I walked into the centrally-heated house. I asked for the jumper to be removed – the dog stopped scratching within 10 minutes. The dog also messed on the upstairs landing carpet; it was allowed to sleep on the owners' bed. It barked at people passing by the house from inside and outside the house and was unpredictable with other dogs. This was a little dog that liked to be in control – and had been allowed to think of itself as ruling the roost.

Now not all this behaviour was down to separation anxiety, but it certainly had a lot to do with it.

I will explain a little more about **separation anxiety**.

We humans take a puppy home and treat it like one of us, because we don't understand how dogs work. We let the dog become attached to its new mother or father and then we go to work and shut the door. The dog starts to whine desperately, and will try to get out of where it is trapped, scratching, digging, chewing…

It has not yet learned to be independent.

I have read lots of books which offer all sorts of different advice such as making sure your dog is well exercised, getting a dog-sitter or dog walker, de-sensitising the dog to the clues that you are going out and so on. One female TV trainer told a lady dog owner: 'take your clothes on and off repeatedly. Put your make-up on but don't go out. Clean your teeth but don't go out. Spray your perfume in the room.'

This is the biggest load of bull I've seen since I was down in the cowshed. It took 10 weeks to get limited results. These people haven't a clue how a dog's mind works, even though they claim to be experts.

The solution is to **wean the dog off the owner**. To do this the owner must, like sheep and deer, drive the dog away. The owner must start to control the space in the house and not let the dog follow them around. This should not be done by closing a door on a dog, but by using blocking and a threat/ challenge exercise (see the General and the Sentry) and removing all affection from the dog for about two weeks so that it sinks in.

The dog needs to become an individual. Simply closing the door between yourself and a dog does not do this: it sees the door simply as a barrier and will wait for it to open and then resume their position close beside you.

By using this method everywhere in the house you force the dog away from you and make it become independent.

People have said to me 'But I don't want to stop giving it love and affection because I don't want it to hate me if I keep pushing it away'.

I have to explain to them that cuddling and loving them is a human thing. When you make the dog independent it looks up to you as a higher rank. The bond between you actually becomes deeper because finally you are acting like a dog and the dog understands what you want and obeys you.

I love my dogs and give them lots of fuss when I want to. However I will revert back to being a Drill Sergeant if they step out of line.

It is difficult for many owners to get the balance right between discipline and affection. I explain it by using a military parallel.

Soldiers do not share all their facilities. The officers have a separate Mess, as do the sergeants and NCOs. There are reasons for this. Respect and obedience.

If the rank and file mixed socially with officers off duty they would lose respect for them. Familiarity can breed contempt. The soldiers might then hesitate to carry out an order which could cost them their lives. They have to rely on the officer's training, experience and higher rank to make the right decision and ensure it is obeyed.

Dogs that are mollycoddled are far more likely to have no respect for their owner. They think **they** are in charge and can do whatever they like.

It's called tough love.

Dogs need rules, leadership and direction.

Trail of destruction

Bo the German Shepherd/Lurcher cross had severe separation anxiety. When left alone she would drool badly and then decided to try to scratch and chew through the wooden door. It is one of the worst cases of damage I have seen. The whole section of door had been chewed away.

CHAPTER 13
Personal space

We all have our own
personal space.

We try to keep people at
arm's length when meeting
someone for the first time.
If a stranger comes within
that distance, you may
start to feel uncomfortable
as they are invading your
personal space.

You may try to move away or you may
physically push them away if you feel
threatened. If you are in a confined space
such as a lift where you are unable to move
away, you will face away from strangers,
avoid eye contact and study the ceiling
or the very interesting shoes you have
on. You are displaying avoidance signals.

People also show avoidance when
walking along the street. If a woman
sees someone coming in the opposite
direction, she will quickly make several
decisions. If the subject approaching
is a male and she does not know him,
she is likely to avoid eye contact.
If she does not want to walk directly
past him, she may cross the road to
give herself a **safe distance** from him.
Most pavements are narrow and force
people into others' safe space so
we adopt avoidance behaviour to show
that we do not want any confrontation.

Dogs also have personal space and will
try to maintain it.

They do it with visual and vocal signals.
Let me give you an example.

You are walking past a dog. You hear
a growl. What do you do? Well, most
people would move away because
they understand the dog is giving
them a warning not to come any closer.
The dog sees you as a threat and is
saying **"back off or I may bite you"**.
What you will not have seen is the fact
that the dog has been watching you and
has waited until you have come into its
personal space. Only then does it growl
to tell you to back off. If you go closer,
the next signal may be a baring
of teeth and a growl. The dog is saying
**"look I warned you and you still
keep approaching me. These are the
teeth that will bite you."** It may bark
a warning, snarl or even make a mock
charge to get you to turn tail. Small dogs
often make little mock charges if they
feel threatened.

Remember: the dog does not want
to fight you. If at all possible it wants to
run away when it sees a threat. If a dog
gets injured in the wild, it is likely to die
because it won't be able to hunt, kill or
defend itself. It is in the interests of the
pack that everyone stays fit and healthy
so fighting over rank or food is not
encouraged. Much of the threatening
behaviour is bravado. Dogs raise their
hackles to make them seem larger and
more threatening, lift their tail and fluff
that out, then show how big their teeth
are and how brave they are. The idea
is to put you off, and prevent a full on
tooth and claw fight. They learn to stop
fighting when the opponent shows
submission and moves away.

By using the same threat/challenge technique you can make the dog stay out of your personal space and establish a higher rank. You communicate with the dog on a dog level. The dog understands straight away because you are simulating dog behaviour.

When you can control your own personal space and get a dog to respect that space by giving it the right signals, it becomes easy to control all the space in your house and you start to become the pack leader. Too many owners use doors and the leash to control the movement of their dog. It doesn't need to be that way.

GET INTO GOOD HABITS

DOGS GET INTO BAD HABITS AND SO DO THEIR OWNERS.

When I have worked with a dog and the owner, I usually have to spend TWICE as long training the owner as I do the dog.

Some owners will follow my techniques until they think the dog is 'fixed'.

They go back to their bad habits and let the discipline slide.

Then they wonder why the dog is misbehaving.

If someone calls me a few months after a training session I ask them a few questions and usually they admit they have relaxed their rules and the dog has taken advantage.

Dogs are like children. If you give them an inch they will continually try to push the boundaries.

CHAPTER 14
Food aggression

People often say to me: 'We do all the things you are supposed to do like go through doors first and make them sit and wait for their food and we always eat first – but the dog is still misbehaving'.

My reply is usually in the form of a question. "Are you telling me these methods don't work?"

It is the reasoning behind these theories which I am at odds with. It credits a dog with more intelligence than it deserves and doesn't look at the problem from the dog's point of view.

Let's deal with the sitting and waiting for food bit. In fact, let's take the case of a trainer on the television in the UK who went to see a family with two beautiful Cocker spaniels with a severe food aggression problem.

I warn you that this is a sad story that ends in unnecessary death and sorrow.

The family had two young daughters and two dogs. The dogs would eat their own food and then steal the food from the family as well, taking food from the hands of the children if they were sitting in front of the TV or continually jumping up at the dinner table to try to get food from the table. The family would sit with their elbows splayed outwards to stop the dogs reaching the food. This would be accompanied by continuous barking.

Enter the TV trainer.

She maintains that the dogs' food is boring which is why they want your human food. Stick with me and I will show you how to make their food more exciting and then use Positive Reinforcement to change how the dogs react to you when you are eating.

And out come the chicken pieces.

I am laughing my head off at this point. Really? Do you think you can stop these dogs being food aggressive by waving a bit of chicken under their noses?

The dogs' dry food was supplemented with something cooked up on the stove and lots of ahhs and umms and **"smell this, now doesn't that smell more appetising? Mmmm lovely"**.

Then came the 'training'. She sat the dog on a mat by the door and got it to wait for scraps of chicken. Soon the dog waited until she gave the release command. **Et voilà! There – you have your dogs rehabilitated. Fantastic. I will be in touch in a few weeks to see how you are getting on.**

But unfortunately that is **not** what happened.

What happened is one of the dogs wanted food from one of the girls and saw the girl as an equal. It fought her over the food resource and bit her four times. She needed a visit to the local hospital for treatment.

The father called the trainer on her mobile phone to tell her what happened and was told the dog was incurable and dangerous and should be put down.

At this point my laughter had turned to anger.

Worse was to follow.

The father took the dog to the vet and had it put to sleep. The film crew then filmed him carrying the body of his dead dog into his back garden to bury it.

By this time I had tears in my eyes.

I could not sleep that night. I knew I could have saved that dog. How could a professional trainer have so completely misunderstood how dogs work, how they see their home, their humans, their food resources? How could she have decided, over the phone, to condemn a dog to death?

This is how I would have handled it.

The situation
If dogs think they are equal or higher in rank to humans they will challenge them for any food. With two dogs in the house there was already competition between them. Spaniels can be aggressive, especially over food.

I should know, as that is how I ended up with Jack, my own Cocker spaniel. I saved him from a lethal injection after he had repeatedly bitten his previous owners.

You may have problems: -

1 If you do not have a clear ranking in the pack

2 If you do not control the space inside your house

3 If you cannot control your dog on and off-lead

4 If your dog does not see you as higher in rank. It may challenge you and try to control you with a nip.

I am not advising you to nip your dogs to control them. There are other effective methods.

1 Establish rank. You do this by controlling space

2 Establish control over the food sources – in a way the dog understands

3 Make clear to the dogs that your children are under your protection. Just as in the wild, you will protect your offspring and drive off any threat, using violence if necessary. PLEASE NOTE: I am not advocating beating up your dog in any way. It is the threat of attack which is implanted into the dog's brain.

I use threats and challenges all the time with dogs. Parents use the same methods with children. If used correctly they are very effective. Used badly, they can become a disaster. Just watch the clueless parents on the **Supernanny** programmes.

Dogs are no different. They use warnings, threats and challenges all the time as well: a growl, a baring of teeth, a bark…

I am going to address the food problem later because that is not the cause of the problem. The cause is lack of leadership.

When I walk into a house, I walk in as a pack leader. I do not greet the dog.

I take control of the house space by using the Sentry and General technique.

When I have shown the owner how to do this, I will then explain why it is so important. Dogs prefer to follow a leader. It makes their life a lot simpler. Once you have established yourself at the top of the pecking order, it is easy to maintain this rank during the everyday routine of caring for your dog.

I explain how dogs compete for and protect food. If they have food in a bowl and they want to signal to another dog to keep away they will lower their head over the bowl and the ears will go back. They will start to stare and growl and maybe even curl a lip and show their teeth. If the other dog approaches and comes too close, they will launch into a charge and possibly a snapping attack.

The dog is giving out a series of warnings, each more aggressive than the last.

My approach is to communicate with the dog so that the dog thinks that when I approach it I am not going to **steal** its food bowl, I am going to **add** to its food bowl. I turn from a thief to a provider.

The next thing I am going to do is to make clear to the dog that **ALL** the food in the house belongs to me. In fact, everything in the house is mine. There are no dog beds, dog toys or dog food in my house, it is all mine until I indicate to the dogs that they can have it.

From thief to provider

For some reason people fill a bowl with dog food and then try to take away the bowl as the dog is eating. Where is the logic in this?

I start with an empty bowl.

I offer the dog a few morsels from my hand. From a crouching position I will then drop a few pieces into the bowl and put it down in front of me. I allow the dog to approach and eat the food until the bowl is empty.

I then wait for the dog to look up at me. When it does so I lean forward and drop a little more food into the bowl.

I wait for the dog to eat it and look at me again.

As soon as it does this, I lean forward, take the bowl away slowly, drop a little more food into the bowl and stare at the dog. Usually the dog will sit down. If it doesn't do this the first time don't worry. It is not that important. To get the dog to sit I will raise my hand above its head and click my fingers. It is amazing how many dogs will just sit down without a command.

I continue to feed the dog with a few morsels and start to leave my hand on the bowl while it is eating so that it gets used to seeing my hand there and that I take and replace the dog's bowl quite often. The dog is starting to see me as a food provider, not a thief.

Another exercise I would use is to challenge the dog over food.

Food challenge exercise

I offer a morsel of dried food to the dog from an open palm.

Then I stand sideways on with my legs apart, and drop a titbit between my feet. By standing over the food you are simulating the guarded posture of a dog and if you slightly crouch and lower your head while standing and staring at the dog you will convey visual threat signals to the dog. If the dog ignores these and starts to move towards the food, use your knee or shin to nudge it away from the food and correct with a vocal warning as well.

Soon you will be able to throw titbits on the floor and the dog will wait for you to give it permission because it does not want to provoke an attack. You will use threat and mock attack signals to get the dog to leave the food and acknowledge the food as yours until you give it permission to have it.

After these exercises I would take control of the work surfaces and table tops to stop the dogs jumping up.

Baiting the trap

Place a titbit on the edge of the table where the dog can see and smell it. Use a high value treat. Small pieces of cheese or sausage are always a good bet.

Stand within arm's length of the treat. If the dog jumps up or goes to snatch the treat you move straight in and barge the dog away with your knee or thigh.

Add in a low short sharp **"NO!"** or **"A!"** and you will quickly take control of the surface and the dog sees the surfaces as off limits.

These three exercises will help you to take control of the food resources, but in my opinion it is **essential** that you are in control of your house space for all this to work.

By using the Sentry and General technique of blocking and threat/ challenge you control a dog and establish a higher rank. You will become a pack leader.

URBAN MYTH

EATING FIRST MAKES YOU THE DOG'S PACK LEADER.

RUBBISH!

Dogs are scavengers and opportunists. They don't really care whether you eat first or not at all. All they are concerned about is "Is there any left for me?" They will wait for as long as it takes until you move away from the food.

Clients often tell me that their dogs won't touch their food until given the command. The dog sees the food as being in your possession until you give the command and walk away.

It's more to do with you standing over the food and staring at them rather than seeing you as in command.

CHAPTER 15
Staring

CHAPTER 15
Staring

CHAPTER 15

Everyone seems to have an opinion on staring.

During my research for this book I wasted several precious hours reading various theories from professionals and the public. These ranged from "your dog is psychic" to "don't stare at a strange dog or it will attack you".

One owner thought the reason her dog appeared to be staring at the wall was because it could see ghosts. OK, these are the most extreme ones I could find, but even trainers get it wrong.

One trainer's advice was to avoid any trainer that stared at dogs. How they communicated with a dog by not looking at them is a mystery to me. I also found a spoof video with some Australian female dog trainers mocking Cesar Millan's method of using a stare to control a dog. They only used treat training which would be useless with the aggressive dogs that Cesar is asked to deal with. In my opinion these people were ignorant of how dogs act and shouldn't really be dog trainers at all.

Major pet welfare organisations advise new owners of rescue dogs not to stare at them. Why? In case they feel intimidated? Bizarre advice but it is there in black and white.

I stare at every dog I meet without exception.

At some point within the first 10 minutes of a one-to-one training session I will stare at the dog. Its reaction tells me the state of mind of that dog and tells me which methods I need to use to treat it.

If I don't stare, it might treat me as an equal and jump all over me because it sees me as a playmate.

I am not an equal, I am of higher rank, and it needs to know this.

An aggressive dog may think it is okay to bite humans to make them go away and try to bite me when I arrive to deal with it.

In the case of an over-friendly jumping dog I want to establish that I am of senior rank; the easiest and quickest way is to use a knee bump to claim your personal space and then the 'parent stare'. Dogs use exactly the same signals to threaten.

The combination of staring, lowering the head and a low growl is a threat.

A dog sitting and looking at you is not threatening; they are most likely just looking for a sign from you about what you are going to do next because **sitting down is a submissive position**. However if that dog is fixating on you with its mouth closed it might just be waiting for you to get within range.

Pip is staring at Jack and Jack is avoiding eye contact and keeping out of his personal space

Maggie the 1 year old English American Bulldog was fearful of humans and had nipped someone. I stared her down and she hid behind her owner and then under the dining table

Staring, ears back, lip curl showing teeth meaning keep your distance

If a dog jumps on me, wanting to play when I walk into a house, I will use a knee bump and stare to say to it in dog language "I am not your playmate, your friend or your equal, I am a senior rank and I demand that you show me the proper respect and keep out of my personal space until I give you a signal that you may approach and sniff me with all four feet on the floor".

That will be the dog's reward, by the way; the privilege of being allowed into my personal space to sniff me.

No dog needs a treat for not jumping up!
I say to my clients that if their dog jumps up on me when I enter their house it is the equivalent of me walking in, throwing my arms around the nearest person and saying "come on, let's play, I'm your new best friend".

I would quickly find myself out on the street again!

A dog with aggressive tendencies must be made to think that I am bigger, stronger and prepared to take it on in a fight.

The most aggressive dogs, the ones which are caged up snarling and barking when I enter the room, are the ones I don't say a word to.

I walk up to the cage and stare at the dog. I need to intimidate this dog. I want it to think that instead of backing away like other humans I am going to see its threats for what they are – mostly bravado.

I want this dog to think that if it bites me I am going to attack and may kill it. I won't, of course – I am just messing with its head and using its basic instincts to change its behaviour and the way it thinks about humans.

This is how it goes in the dog's head. For the purposes of brevity I will assume a female is the handler. No offence intended!

- Now what the hell does my owner want now?

- Okay I know the sit, that's easy but now she is moving away. I really want to be close to her but she is staring down at me and lowering her head and barking out a low warning bark. Those are threat signals!

- Well I'll go towards her anyway – oh crikey now she is charging towards me and barking really aggressively. I'll sit again and wait for her to say I can get close again.

- Ah now she's giving me that nice high voice tone I get when she is pleased with me so I will go to her but give her a low wag and keep my head down so she knows I am submissive. Ooh bonus, a bit of food!

Most trainers and owners assume the dog is performing for a treat. It is not. You have given the dog several threat signals both vocal and visual and the dog does not want to provoke an attack from you.

If you use the General and Sentry threat/challenge method you can achieve a sit/stay in two minutes. The dog understands because you are using a dog technique on a dog.

Dogs rely on lots of visual signals to communicate with other dogs probably 90% visual and 10% vocal.

Humans tend to be the opposite; we are far more vocal than dogs are maybe 90% vocal. It's not a great combination really, is it?

By studying and simulating their signals I have been able to get dogs to do things in minutes when conventional treat training takes forever.

One of my most powerful tools is the parent stare.

Try it; you'll be amazed at the results.

You will be familiar with the parent stare

It's the one your mum used when she was fed up of your whingeing and she wanted you to take her seriously. She would go perfectly still, lower her head slightly, narrow the eyes, purse her lips and the eyes would bore through you. Her voice would lower and through gritted teeth she would use your full name **"Adrian Howe, go to bed NOW!"**

When I was a small child nobody told me that those were threat signals. I learned by experience.

Teachers use the same technique. One retired teacher said to me **"I can't believe how simple that is. For years all I had to do was stare at a child and raise an eyebrow to get it to behave and now you are showing me it works with dogs as well."**

CHAPTER 16
Transporting dogs

I once went to rehabilitate a dog which had been delivered to its new owner in a crate in the back of an estate car by a rescue centre volunteer.

The metal crate had been covered over with a blanket to keep the dog quiet, and the dog had arrived panting and distressed. The volunteer ventured a theory that the dog probably did not like travelling in cars.

I was appalled that a rescue centre which is supposed to be looking after an animal's welfare would treat a dog like this.

It was summer. The crate was covered and consequently the air supply in the cage was restricted. The temperature was rising with every mile and it was obvious to me that the heat and lack of fresh air was making the dog very distressed.

Some people are so stupid it beggars belief.

Several weeks previously I had ridden in the back of an estate car with a dog which barked at everything that went by the window. I had climbed into the boot of the car to be with the dog and correct it when necessary. The owners were sitting in the front seats with their windows partially open so they were getting a nice breeze.

Their dog and I however were toasting nicely in the back, struggling for air and overheating. The dog was panting and slobbering and I am sure this added to the dog's distress. I was sweating like a Geordie in a maths test. I quickly shouted out to get some windows open to give us a decent air supply.

So if you are taking your dog anywhere make sure they have an adequate air supply and the temperature is not going to cause your dog distress. Overheating and heatstroke can happen very quickly and there are many documented cases of dogs dying in vehicles with closed windows and no water.

I often have my dogs in the back of the car when I visit clients. If I stop for any length of time I leave all the windows partially open ensuring a flow of air through the car. They have a bowl of water in the car and I use a silver reflective shield and a large sheet to keep the sun from radiating into the interior. I regularly check on the dogs, the water and the car temperature and let them out for a run as soon as I can. Where possible I will park in the shade as well.

One thing I noticed with my three dogs is that the ranking in the house is carried into the car. Pip was top dog and he would lie down where he wanted and the other two would sit or lie down facing away from him, showing avoidance.

Not all dogs are as lucky as Harry Price in his bespoke mobile kennel complete with ramp

Because there is not much room for three dogs, Jack, the lowest-ranked and youngest would sometimes bury his head into the corner to avoid confrontation with Pip. Sometimes I would have to tell Pip to move if he started growling at the other two. They display the same behaviour as humans do in a crowded lift – avoidance.

If you have several dogs you may find that you need to crate them separately to avoid confrontation. It is a question of personal space. Dogs like to have theirs and will growl if it is invaded.

One client of mine always loaded the top dog into the car first and it would then bark and growl at the second dog. I suggested that it was trying to defend its personal space and to try reversing the dog loading or crating them separately.

I once went to see a family with a Staffordshire bull terrier with some behavioural problems, one of which was the desire to sit in the front seat of the car. The lady of the house was pregnant and the car was a two-door coupé. She found that it was getting more difficult to get into the back of the car as the baby grew inside her.

The thought of one of my dogs sitting up front while a human sat in the back made me chuckle. I got in the back with the dog, which kept trying to leap through the gap between the two front seats. I restrained it with a lead. What they had forgotten to tell me was that the dog, when it got excited, would start passing wind. The windows in the rear of the coupé were of the type that only opened about an inch on the latch.

I had my face pressed to the window trying to get a breath of fresh air from outside and calling for the windows to be opened. My clients sat in the front of the car chuckling.

I corrected the dog with a mixture of lead corrections, vocal corrections and a simulation of a nip from a senior dog, using a finger poke. We drove around the neighbourhood for 10 or 15 minutes and initially the dog was whining and trying to jump through the gap. This calmed down to the occasional whimper. The owners reported later that by using all the simple methods I had shown them, they had a dog which had started to behave totally differently and showed them much more respect.

One Border Collie rescue dog was an absolute nightmare in the back of a car. It would run from one side to the other, throw itself at the window and bark maniacally at everything that it passed, especially at white vans. My client had only had the dog a short time and it had other serious aggression issues, so I first did some leadership exercises in the house before we ventured out to the car.

I got into the back seat of the car, with the dog in the boot space. I threaded the lead through the bars of the head rest. I had noticed that the dog would lunge across the car until its muzzle hit the window and then start barking crazily, so I shortened the lead to only a foot long. The dog stopped barking. We drove around for 20 minutes, without a sound from the dog. We parked outside the client's house, on a busy road, at school throwing-out time.

We stepped out of the car and waited a few minutes. The dog did not lunge or bark at the children or passing traffic including vans and buses.

Another technique which can be used is to run a long lead (or two tied together) from the dog in the back to the front seats so that a lead tug can be used to correct the dog from the front of the car. For safety's sake it is better to have two people in the car, one person driving so the other can concentrate on the dog.

It just takes kindness, common sense and an awareness of what a dog (and for that matter any living thing) needs: space, air, water and consideration.

One idea I saw recently I thought was brilliant. Someone had frozen some water into a block of ice with the dog's toy and some small treats inside. This will not only help to keep your dog cool on a warm day but give it something to occupy it as well.

OK, I'm ready, let's go!

I made the mistake of leaving the driver's door open and Buster decided that the view from the front seat far outweighed the extra room in the back.

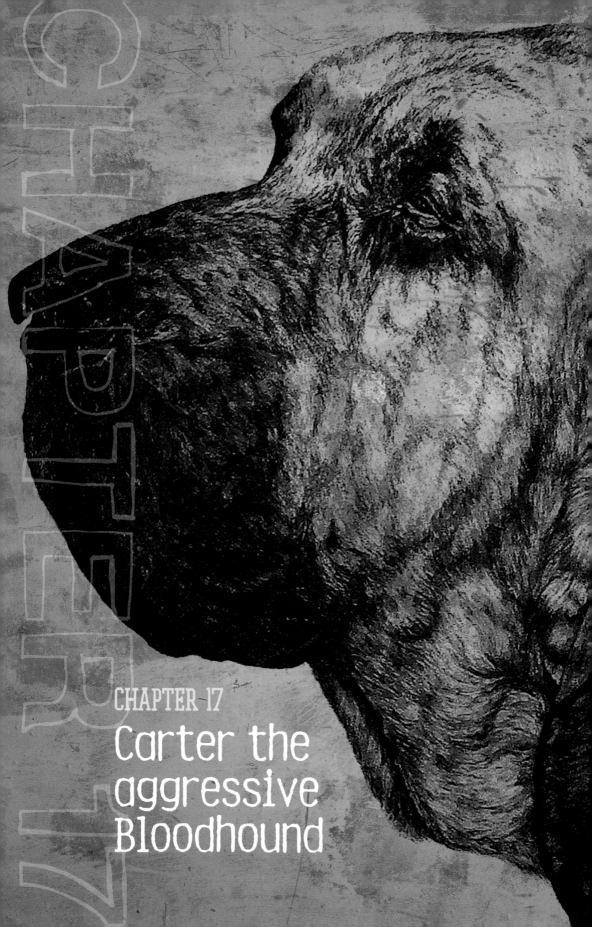

CHAPTER 17

Carter the aggressive Bloodhound

We spent some time searching for a dog behaviourist. It had to be the right one as we had a large two-and-a-half-year-old Champion Bloodhound called Carter, a male weighing in at nine stone that was being particularly difficult. We contacted Ade and booked an appointment on Christmas Eve.

Carter was showing aggression towards me with food, his cage, the van, in the house and especially in the kitchen. He also showed aggression to our five-year-old male Bloodhound but never showed anything to my partner Rob.

Carter is very wilful and stubborn which are part of the breed characteristics and he had shown particular behaviour before but not as bad as this. I had resolved some issues with Carter before, but this last episode seemed to be the result of a neighbour's dog crashing through the hedge into our garden.

When Ade arrived, Carter was in a cage. He growled, barked and stared at him. After talking to us for a minute or two Ade put on gloves and told us to let Carter out. With a certain amount of trepidation we did so. Ade worked calmly with Carter, teaching us how to behave with him, and using body blocks, knee bumps and vocal corrections.

We then let our other male dog in and Ade corrected him quickly and the whole situation stayed under control, so Carter remained calm and relaxed.

Ade offered us a solution in retraining us with new methods.

What Ade did was amazing and has made living with Carter a lot easier. Ade's advice and understanding is invaluable, a no-nonsense approach, but a kind way of teaching for dogs and humans.

It is two years since he came to see us and Carter has just won his 4th Best in Show at a breed show!
Evelyn Burnside

Case history

Carter was caged when I arrived and growled and barked at me, staring aggressively. Logan was kept upstairs. After the initial chat, I asked for the cage to be unlocked. I immediately blocked the cage door with my legs and he backed off. I stood for a few seconds and then let him out. I then used my body to block him into the corner and he sat down showing submission. I explained about taking over space, claiming the house as your own, keeping hands out of the way and using your body to block the dog and challenge it. I blocked Carter from coming into the room and held him there with a stare and then released him. We each had a go and Carter responded well. I showed how to use a knee bump to correct him and use the vocal correction as well.

We did some work at the front door, using the hallway to block him and then went into the lounge. He had a half-hearted little nip at me when I turfed him off the sofa, but apart from that he was well-behaved. I asked for Logan to be brought down and kept Carter under control by not allowing him to jump up on the stair gate, using a knee bump and a vocal correction again. Both dogs were calm and any signs of bad behaviour were quickly corrected. Carter lay down in the lounge and Rob said he had never seen them so calm. Senior dogs will often break up a fight between the lower ranks so by being in charge and taking control you show the dogs that you will not tolerate any fighting between them and that they will be reprimanded.

Rob Manley with Carter and his trophies

Hunting with Bloodhounds is called 'Hunting the Clean Boot' because the hounds hunt the natural body scent of man and not an artificial trail such as aniseed.

Bloodhound Trials are in essence a tracking competition. They are not a hunt with a pack of hounds and a field of mounted or foot followers. The hounds are tested individually on their ability to hunt man. Each hound hunts a different person on a different piece of ground.

The procedure is for the 'runner' (or quarry) to walk a precise prearranged line (marked out for him on a large scale map). The runner leaves an article of clothing e.g. his sock, handkerchief etc., on a flag at the start of the line as a 'smeller' for the hound. After a specific interval of time the hound is taken to the flag by his handler and sets off in pursuit of the runner. Hound and handler will be accompanied by the judge and his assistants who assess the hounds in turn for their hunting prowess.

LOGAN

CHAPTER 18

Behaviourists

I am not going to say what I really think about a lot of behaviourists, canine counsellors and dog trainers. I promised my mother I wouldn't use bad words.

Instead I will list the things they have advised my clients to do to their dogs in order to change their behaviour. I will also paraphrase a few comical stories I have seen in books and magazines.

These people are charging high fees for methods which do not work.

Owners are led to believe it takes a lot of time (and of course money) to change the behaviour of a dog. This is absolutely **not** the case. It can take just minutes to change a dog's behaviour – if you use the correct techniques.

I was reading a book the other day, written by a very famous and fêted dog listener. In it she described how she goes about curing separation anxiety, and gave an example that made me titter. She asked one owner to climb out of her kitchen window and walk around the house to the front door, leaving the dog alone, and rather bemused. The owner was instructed to do this all weekend. Goodness knows what the neighbours thought. I know what I thought:
what a load of tripe!

Separation anxiety is usually caused by dogs attaching themselves to their owners and makes them follow them all the time. The dogs need to be weaned off their owners and taught to become individuals. The owners don't need to take up gymnastics in their own home.

A client asked me to see her Chinese Crested dog because he was impossible to live with. He barked constantly at other dogs (even on the television), he bullied his dog companion, he destroyed expensive wooden Venetian blinds at the front window…

Life was a nightmare.

When I arrived, they told me they had taken the dog to a dog training class – a professional training class, accredited by the Kennel Club, charging fees for training – where he had barked for 20 minutes at the other dogs. They were attending the class to get help. They were all asked to leave, and not come back.

What a disgrace!

I managed to stop the dog barking within minutes and worked through the list of problems presented to me including aggression to other dogs. Within three hours that dog was off-lead with my three dogs on the park.

Well, how do you stop a dog barking? Slow and steady training over a number of weeks? Well, no actually. It's quick and easy.

A quick tug upwards on the lead and a nudge with the knee on the dog's shoulder and a sharp "A" and a stare usually does the trick within about 20 seconds.

Surely something every dog trainer should know?

I remember being asked to see a lady with a Belgian Shepherd. She had already spent £1,000 on dog trainers with no effect: this dog was vicious with both people and other dogs and had no intention of changing its ways. Apparently it had prevented the previous trainer from coming into the house **three times**!

I was obviously very wary. Before my visit, I asked the owner to lock the dog away in the kitchen before I arrived. We chatted for about 10 minutes while the dog barked constantly in the kitchen.

She asked if she should let the dog out.

No, I said, I would go into the kitchen to make its acquaintance.

Her daughter arrived just before I did this. I slowly opened the kitchen door, behind which was a large aggressively barking and growling Belgian Shepherd. Keeping my small rucksack in front of me, I inched into the room. The dog started to back off, still barking. I gradually backed it into the corner of the kitchen and blocked each attempt it made to get past me. I kept nudging it with the bag in front of me and stared down at it, verbally correcting each bark. I eventually backed it right up against the cupboard door. It stopped barking and sat down with a mini-growl. I barked back at it and started to slowly move away, still staring. The dog lay down on the floor and remained quiet.

The owner and her daughter were speechless.

I explained that it had worked because I had faced the dog's challenge. By not backing down, I had shown it that I was prepared to fight, and because I am a much bigger animal, it had shown me submissive body signals by lying down and keeping out of my personal space.

I did have to go back to see the dog a second time. I was able to take it out on the lead without getting attacked, and it also walked the streets with my dogs without a fight. Unfortunately, I got the feeling that the owner was part of the problem – the dog needed someone physically and mentally strong to rehabilitate it fully. It was a lovely-looking dog, large and powerful, but it had lost its way and needed a strong leader.

One owner told me that a trainer at a class had told her that her dog would not do what she wanted **'because her treats were not good enough'**. She should be using cheese or liver sausage. I got her dog to sit and stay within minutes without a treat, without a command, and kept it there with a stare.

Treats do not work for every dog. Trainers who think they do should be in another line of work. A lot of owners do not want to use treats to train their dog. Where does that leave them when all they are offered is treat training?

Another owner told me that during the class they had attended the dog had been fed so many treats that when they got home it vomited all over the floor. Why would anyone feed a dog to such an extent that it was sick?

They stopped going to the classes and searched for a trainer who didn't use treats.

One owner was turned away as they reached the door of the training hall because their dog was already barking. They never got to go in a class at all. Should these trainers be allowed to call themselves trainers and be accredited by the Kennel Club when they can't even stop a dog barking?

Oh and by the way, this 'trainer' advertises herself on the internet as a trainer/behaviourist and has written several books.

A change in training

Dog training needs to see a big change – in method and professionalism.

I have had several clients who were told their dog was **too stupid** to do anything right. A dog I got to obey with no trouble at all. Maybe it was the trainer who was stupid. I shall rephrase that. The trainer **was** stupid. No maybe about it.

People usually don't want to give up on their dogs, even if they are driving them mental with their behaviour. Often they have been given terrible advice by professional trainers and behaviourists.

A client whose dog growled and barked at visitors was advised to ask the visitors to feed the dog treats by hand **'to make it friendly and see you as a source of good things'**. This is an excellent way to get a nervous aggressive dog to bite someone who is already terrified by its snarling and snapping.

Some trainers think that telling a frightened child to give a treat to a growling dog will change the way the dog or the child feel about the other.

In my opinion this is dangerous madness and will end in tragedy for the child or the dog or both.

A client who lives near me with a rescue German Shepherd/husky cross had an hour's worth of leash training with me to stop the dog pulling. Because I only run workshops once a month, they decided to take their dog to a weekly class in the next village. The trainer there refused to allow it to attend classes because it was a rescue dog that my client had only had three weeks "so it might turn nasty in six weeks".

The trainer did not even look at the dog.

I went to see a couple who had adopted a lovely little Jack Russell called Basil. Basil went bonkers at any dog he met, growling, barking, lunging and snapping. They had called a trainer recommended by the rescue centre. She had told them that once the dog had turned aggressive there was no hope for him and they should return him to the centre.

They called me.

I went out to see Basil and within an hour and a half that dog was off-lead in their back garden with my three dogs. It was an easy case for me and the boys.

Another dog condemned by someone with no experience of rehabilitating an unsocialised dog purporting to be a professional.

Another tragedy averted thanks to Pip, Buster and Jack with a little help from me.

CASE HISTORY

Greyhounds

Ex-racing greyhounds can make good pets but you really need to understand their background and be aware of their hunting instincts.

I have been able to help a few owners to rehabilitate their dogs. One lucky dog now known as Zebedee got two new owners called Penny and Mike and this is his story in their words.

Zebedee – Brindle greyhound adopted from the Retired Greyhound Trust by Mike and Penny O'Callaghan in March 2011.

We made three visits to the kennels and fell for Markland Marvel (his racing name) mainly because his coat was in good condition and he was friendly.

We were allowed to have him on loan for the weekend and of course we became hooked and he came to live with us permanently.

You, Ade were our first point of contact for doggy advice and we also attended two other dog training schemes for a brief length of time. Both were useful in getting Zeb to mix with other breeds.

Ex-racing greyhounds have a peculiar life during their racing days; very different from many rescued dogs that have had some degree of domesticity. For greyhounds there has been no house-training; no mixing with other dogs; minimal street walking and no freedom except on the racecourse.

They are very used to being handled by their trainers and walk very well to heel on a lead. Most hounds I have come across are calm, well-natured, gentle and friendly and enjoy a fuss.

They vary greatly in size. Zebedee is 32 kilos and is on the large side. Some are almost like tall whippets.

I do feel like many owners that the breed is different and special. Zebedee is laid-back, sleeps a lot, enjoys his walks and loves his food but he is not greedy. He does not appear interested in toys or balls but I know some greyhounds that are.

House training took a couple of weeks, we were quite vigilant and did not have too many accidents. Night-time was more difficult but by varying the times of his meals we resolved the problem. He always 'asks' to be let out – sometimes in the middle of the night.

He is never left alone for long and has never been destructive but he carried out some thieving the first few days we had him.

A parcel of fresh fish was triumphantly carried out to the garden and although rescued promptly was rendered unsuitable for human consumption. I also caught him returning for **seconds** of flapjack before I had time to move them to a higher level and on one occasion I saw out of the corner of my eye the ham for the ham salad disappearing off the plate and swallowed in one gulp.

We now keep food out of his reach, but he does not interfere when we are having a meal or a snack on our knees.

The R.G.T. advised us to be careful about letting him off the lead, to get him to wear a muzzle and to watch out for small dogs which might appear to him to be a rabbit on a string.

We followed their common sense instructions, but after about six months we set him free while on holiday in Lyme Regis. Zeb was marvellous. We removed his lead, he trotted along with us and if he moved ahead he would wait to see if we were coming. Three years later he is still good.

It took some time for him to accept other dogs. He used to be a bit snappy with most of them, particularly the small ones. (This is sometimes known as 'pecking'. Ed) This has improved over time and while I would never trust him with a tiny dog, he is kinder with them. We always take a muzzle with us and he wears it some of the time. Several hound owners I have met give their dogs freedom all the time and never wear muzzles but you learn which type of hound you own. Horses for courses.

Going to various dog classes helped and so did meeting other dogs on our walks.

The highlight of our activities is the monthly greyhound walk; only greyhounds and their owners. It's a joy to see all the hounds together and they seem pleased to be with their own kind – just like their racing days. Their experiences are many and varied and it is useful to exchange information with the other owners.

Everyone's experience will vary whichever type of breed you own but in the final analysis they are man and woman's best friend and are great fun, good company and a provider of a daily keep-fit routine which keeps us in touch with nature and the changing seasons.

TV time

"Hurry up, Pet Rescue's on in a minute."

CHAPTER 19
The walk

What is a dog walk to a human?

A walk is exercise, fresh air and allowing the dog to go to the toilet. Some owners may interact with their dog by playing games or doing some training but a lot of owners are just leash holders.

A walk to a dog, however, can be many things.

- A scouting party for prey. A lot of dogs will try to chase cats, birds, rabbits, joggers and bikes. Their chase and kill instinct is still active.
- A patrol of the pack territory. Dogs do not fully empty their bladder straight away like humans. They keep a reservoir to mark territory by urinating over the scent of others, and they will do this after sniffing to check who has passed by.
- To meet other members of an extended pack – the doggie friends on the park.

The pack leader decides when to go hunting. The pack detects the scents of other animals that have marked their territory. They can decipher whether that dog scent is male, female, full or neutered, in season or pregnant.

When dogs in a pack meet another animal, they must decide if it is friend or foe. They do this initially by reading its body language. By staying calm and assertive, the pack leader shows that we will greet every dog in a friendly way. If we meet a dog whose owner is not in charge and the dog starts barking and lunging, we will avoid and ignore it.

Dogs greet by sniffing mouths, bottoms and sexual parts and use tail wags and other visual signals to show they are not aggressive.

Calm submissive behaviour

What I want to see is a calm dog with its mouth open, carrying its tail horizontal or lower with big, slow horizontal wags and looking around – not staring. Wanting to sniff is a good sign – dogs that want to attack won't sniff at all. Many owners misinterpret the excited lunging forward of a young dog as an aggressive move but it is usually just to sniff.

Sitting and lying down are submissive positions. A dog lying down on its back is showing total surrender. This is very common with puppies and young or timid dogs. Running away with the tail held low or completely tucked away is a very submissive signal and other signs are holding the tail between the legs and cowering and yelping, sometimes accompanied by a nervous pee.
The yelping does not always mean your dog has been bitten. I have seen dogs that yelp like a scalded cat when another dog just comes near them.

Turning away from an approaching dog or hiding behind the owner is avoidance behaviour. Avoiding eye contact is also a sign the dog doesn't want anything to do with the other dog.

Dogs which lack dog manners can fool other dogs into thinking they are friendly.

I have regularly seen dogs that will approach other dogs tentatively, have a friendly sniff for a few seconds and then suddenly snap at the other dog or even bite and hold on in certain cases. These are usually dogs that have missed out on socialisation when they were young or have been the victim of an attack themselves. They appear to behave for a few seconds and then suddenly snap. If I detect my dogs are nervous about meeting a client's dog I will muzzle the other dog to keep all the dogs safe. Often a dog with issues will go into complete submission when muzzled and just stand with its head low, tail tucked under the body and in some cases shivering. I worked out that these dogs feel defenceless when muzzled and try to show my dogs submission so that they won't be attacked. It takes them a while to work out my dogs are not interested in fighting them as they are usually sitting by the gate waiting to get out of the garden away from the aggressive dog.

Submissive behaviour

Here I am with Pip and Buster working with Tess, a very aggressive Jack Russell. Tess had already tried to attack Pip and Buster. She was corrected with a firm lead tug, vocal correction and stare.

Tess then had to choose a different behaviour as she could not move away from the 3 of us. She chose to go into avoidance. You can see Tess is facing away from Pip and Buster, she is lying down, leaning away and her tail is down. You might just make out that she is looking sideways to keep an eye on Pip. Pip has already growled at her and then decided to ignore her and allow her to calm down.

There is a dog conversation going on here but it is mostly using visual signals.

QUESTIONS
TO ASK TRAINERS

What is your full-time job?

If they don't solve problem dogs full-time they may not have the experience you need.

Don't be fooled by people who earn their living from running group training classes with masses of treats, it is no guarantee of skill.

How many dogs did you see individually last year?
That is, not in group sessions.

If it is only one or two a week and they are charging a lot, it may be wise to ask why?

How many sessions do you think it would take to cure my dog?

One session of two to three hours is usually all I need to fix most problems.

Do you actually work with the dog or do you just tell us what to do?

Some trainers/behaviourists will not work with dogs that are even slightly aggressive and may sit and talk to you for three or four hours but never go near your dog. Avoid them. Some will just 'assess' your dog and write a report. Avoid like the plague.

Can you guarantee a quick result?

If you cannot see an immediate improvement and a calming of your dog's attitude during one session then do not employ them.

Do you have any reviews on an independent review site?

Like any business, current reviews are a guide to the professionalism and skills of the trainer/behaviourist. If they only have a few undated reviews on their personal web site or a handful on an independent site then their clients can't be that impressed with them.

Do you think aggression in dogs is caused by diet?

If you have an aggression problem with either dog-to-dog or dog-to-human, it is behavioural and nothing to do with their diet. Changing a dog's diet is not going to stop it trying to bite visitors. It is common sense.

Do you shout at dogs?

I have heard from several of my clients who employed someone that entered the house and started shouting at the dog straight away. Avoid. I usually do not say a word to start with.

CHAPTER 20
The recall

The first thing you have to ask yourself is why the dog will not come back when called.

Let's consider a few possibilities.
If the dog is not let off the leash much then it will want freedom to run, sniff, mark territory and blow off steam rather than walking at a slow human pace.

It may be trapped inside a house or small garden all day and feel bored.

A dog meets its own kind on the park. Other dogs are more interesting than humans so running off to meet new friends on the other side of the park is fun especially as the owner sometimes runs after them shouting which might appear to the dog as excited 'barking'.

A lot of people take their dog to the park, let them off lead and virtually ignore the dog for the rest of the time on the park. They talk to other owners, walk for two laps or 20 minutes and then put the lead on the dog and go home.

The dog learns that arriving at the park gate after two laps means it is going home and it doesn't want to go home. It wants to play.

So it jumps around just out of reach and this behaviour suddenly gets it a lot of attention from its owner.

The owner may panic or get frustrated and angry if the dog does not come back immediately and this comes out in the increasingly desperate calls to the dog.

The dog thinks it is going to get punished when it goes back and is even more reluctant to return. A red-faced, eyes-bulging, ranting owner will display all the threat signals a dog needs to make it keep well away.

If a dog sees its owner as equal in rank there is no reason to follow the owner or to come back when called. The owner will still be there in five or 20 minutes so why bother? Often when a dog comes back there is little reward for it.

So you can see there are many reasons for a dog not to come back to its owner when called.

What is the answer?
The owner has to become the pack leader and more exciting than everything else. You want the dog to think several things such as:-

My pack leader is moving away from me so I need to follow or I might lose him.

I might get a nice treat or favourite toy when I go racing back.

I might get lots of praise and fuss.

Maybe I will get a quick massage. Some dogs love this sort of attention.

I am going to chase after my pack leader because he is running away and I like to chase, plus he might have found something good to chase.

Just relying on treats is daft. What happens if you forget or run out of treats or your dog is not hungry or interested in treats? Your dog should want to be with you whether you have treats or not.

Using a long lead to teach recall. A long lead is also useful to allow a dog some freedom without it being able to run off.

Before I even start the recall exercises I get the owner to carry out a few core techniques in the house. The General and Sentry exercise is essential to get your dog to look at you as being in charge and its pack leader.

I block, barge and bark then use the parent stare.

I take control of the house and the front door and then take command of the walk and that dog then becomes a follower and I am their leader.

When you have done all that, the recall becomes easier because you are building a bond with your dog, and you start to understand and respect each other.

You can build a good basic recall in the house and garden by calling the dog's name with the command "come". Use a high voice tone to make it more exciting.

You can play hide and seek with your dog. If you get someone to hold the dog inside the house and then hide in the garden or vice versa you can then call the dog, they release the dog and the dog finds you. It is fun for the dog and the owner. The dog doesn't realise it is a training method but enjoys it all the same. If you are on your own you can make the dog sit and stay until you call it. This really makes the dog want to be with you.

Because I don't use a lot of praise or any treats during a normal day, I can save it all for when I am out on the park. It becomes much more powerful. If I call a dog to me on the park I will always give it some praise and a fuss so that it learns it will get a reward when it comes to me.

When I teach the recall with a new dog I occasionally use the long lead, 10 metres of rope, which means if the dog doesn't recall I can reel it in. Even if it runs off, I only need to get to within 10m to get hold of the rope.

I will often start by having the dog on the long lead and changing direction by 90 degrees every 30 metres or so. Usually the dog will be in front so when I change direction it will be behind me again. I change direction and make them follow me, rather than the other way around.

Another exercise would be to start with the lead about two metres long and walk backwards so that the dog follows me as I say "come on then" as I walk. After several metres I turn and walk and the dog usually trots along beside me. I might start to trot and then change direction, calling to the dog as I turn to get it to follow. I will stop and start, change direction, change speed and try to interact with the dog so that I become more interesting to it because I am interested in it!

I make it sit, I walk backwards away from it and call it after a few seconds and keeping moving. It doesn't have to be like conventional training classes where you have to have the dog sit in front of you and you have to do things by numbers. I find that so boring and unnatural and no doubt so does the dog.

I find I can make a dog come to me just by crouching down to their level as they find humans far more inviting if they are on the same eye level as you. This is really powerful. Clients are amazed when halfway through the session I just crouch down with open arms and I am surrounded by my dogs and theirs, all wanting some attention.

Here are some more exercises:

1   **Ask** a friend/partner to hold the dog by the collar at a starting distance of 10 metres apart, working your way up to 50 metres or more.

    Stand up straight, wave your arms wide so that the dog can see and focus on some movement, say "Buster, come!" in a high, sing-song friendly voice so the dog takes notice of you and clap twice to help the dog focus on a sound as well. Your friend releases the dog, then as the dog approaches, you praise the dog. Then praise some more.

    You are turning this into a positive experience for the dog instead of a "come here I want to go home you blasted animal!"

    Practise to get the dog to sit so that it doesn't knock you over as it runs up to you. I use the long leash for this to be able to catch the dog even when the distractions prove too much, for instance kids, footballers, other dogs.

    You can do this exercise in the home and in the garden or park using the dog's normal dried food as an added incentive. This way the dog has to work for its food. Use high praise for the dog; act pleased to see him when he comes to you.

2   **Let** the dog see you go behind a bush/tree so you are just out of sight and call the dog. Your friend releases the dog and he runs to find you. You may call the dog again after a few seconds to help him focus on where you are. Repeat until you are happy with the exercise.

Let the dog see you go out of sight, but then hide yourself so you are not immediately visible. This is to make the dog search with eyes, ears and nose to find you.

Make it into a great game with the dog and make sure he gets lots of praise and/or a treat when he finds you. You must make yourself into the most irresistible thing in his world. Go in the woods and when the dog is sniffing somewhere, slip out of sight and hide.

Do not call the dog; let it panic and rush around to find you with eyes, ears and nose. If it can't find you straight away then give a short whistle or call its name once. Then wait. Once you have 'lost yourself' a few times, your dog will start to keep an eye on you much more and stay closer to you.

Call the dog and run away. Get him to chase you. Praise when he catches up to you. Dogs love a game of chase.

3   **Command** the dog to sit or lie down. Move away a few yards and recall. Praise the dog. Repeat exercise and slowly increase the distance from the dog up to maybe 100 metres. If the dog gets up to follow go towards it and give a verbal command "Buster DOWN", with a hand sign.

Repeat and repeat, a little every day, 10-20 minutes stops the dog getting bored. A couple of short blasts on a dog whistle in addition to the verbal command will get the dog to respond to the whistle. I used a dog whistle with Buster which he learnt in two days with cheese as an added incentive. Buster tends to explore the whole of the park or field that we are in, sometimes disappearing for five minutes in the long grass. I use a lip whistle with Jack.

Repeat several times on the walk; put the dog on the leash for one minute then release.

The dog will get used to coming back but not going home, the idea is to get it so that he doesn't associate the recall with going home but just something nice, a treat, fuss, praise, a favourite toy etc.

I will let you into a secret now.
I watched a horse whisperer do a join-up exercise in a ring once to make a horse follow him by driving it away. It got me thinking. Would the same technique work with a dog because they are both herd/pack animals?

The most common question I get asked about the recall is this. If my dog only comes back after five or 10 minutes what should I do? Should I praise it for coming back or should I tell it off?

If I praise it there is no reason why it won't take forever to come back every time but on the other hand if I tell it off surely that will make it reluctant to come back to me again?

The answer is to neither praise nor punish. The answer is to chase that dog away.

As the dog is (finally) returning I wait until it is 20 metres away and start to chase it away from me. I run towards it shouting and staring at it with a lowered head. I am trying to look threatening and make the dog run away from me.

I run for 15 yards and abruptly turn and calmly walk away. Usually when I take a glance over my shoulder the dog is standing absolutely dumbfounded and will start to follow me. I repeat this once or twice more and now I really have the dog's attention.

I have driven it away from MY pack as punishment and it now it desperately wants to join my pack so it trots up showing submissive signals, a low wagging tail and its head held low and maybe even crouching a little. I then crouch down and welcome it back into the fold.

It may seem unbelievable but incredibly it works. The dog tends to hang around you closer than ever before.

Common errors on the recall.
Just shouting the dog's name and not giving the command as well.

Standing still when a distance away from the dog. Dogs detect movement at a distance; they can't see you very well if you stay still so wave your arms.

Not being loud enough with the command. Wind can carry your voice away. Bark it out.

Not giving enough praise and high-pitched voice as the dog approaches. The last few yards are the most important.

A lack of practice.
Practice makes permanent.

Client review

Ade came to help us with our rescue Lurcher Alfie, who jumps at the door, runs to the door, pulls on the lead and runs off.

After only a few weeks, it is like having a different dog in the house, and outside. The walks are now relaxing and my shoulder doesn't hurt. Ade has taught us to trust Alfie, and that has really worked, watching him run is now an absolute pleasure, and he comes back every time (not always when called, but he does come back).

No more running to the door like a berserker... It is very hard to describe the difference this has made to our life with our dog. It is amazing!!!

We were sceptical at first, but within five minutes we knew the techniques work. Absolutely unbelievable.

Our little lurcher Lennie also no longer piddles in the house. Sorted within a week... Again, what a difference this has made!
Patricia Freeborn

CHAPTER 21

Hook restriction therapy

Hook restriction therapy.

Nothing to do with Peter Pan but definitely belongs in Never-Never land.

Hook restriction therapy is a technique used to deal with excitable behaviour with visitors.

A hook is secured into a skirting board and a lead is permanently attached to it.

Pre-stuffed Dental Kongs are stored in the fridge.

When the doorbell rings the dog will jump on the furniture and visitors and may bark non-stop or constantly want to play.

With this method you attach the dog to the lead on the hook and giving him a Kong filled with food before opening the door.

Apparently this works after a few MONTHS of training and has been used on thousands of dogs.

Is this what you want to do to your dog?

Do you want to chain your dog to your skirting board and distract it with food every time someone comes to your door?

I think someone is having us on.

I have three dogs. Would I have to chain all three up and give them a food distraction EVERY time someone came to my door? They would be the fattest dogs in the village.

I have heard some absurd things in my time but this one has to be in the Top Ten.

I use the General and the Sentry method to stop the dog getting over-excited. I take control of the area around the door and by doing so I reduce the excitement by 90%.

It usually takes less than an hour to train the dog and owner and if you stick with the method it is permanent.

If a trainer or behaviourist mentions Hook restriction therapy walk away and save yourself a lot of time and money as they clearly do not understand dogs.

CHAPTER 22
Trainers' sayings

The things people say!

Here's a selection of the bad and ugly things my clients have been told by various dog trainers, behaviourists, pet counsellors and dog listeners.

Ignore the bad behaviour and reward the good.

My client had a dog that would not stop barking. So the trainer let the dog bark for the entire hour of the class.

This theory doesn't stand up to one moment of scrutiny. If you ignored a child's bad behaviour and rewarded the good you would be a long time waiting. You are virtually asking them to guess. You should teach the child right from wrong and what is allowed and what is forbidden. You must do the same with your dog.

It's your fault your dog is like this.

Translation: I haven't a clue how to fix your dog so the easiest thing is to blame you and you won't come back next week. Then it's not my problem!

You could send it back to the rescue centre or have it put to sleep.

Translation: Your dog scares me and I don't want to go near it as I don't know what I am doing.

Your dog has obviously got a hereditary defect.

Translation: Nothing I can do can change this dog so I will blame its parents rather than own up to my lack of knowledge.

When I worked with the same dog I had no problems with it.

At last! Something Henry can do!

A client was struggling to get her dog to do anything and the trainer couldn't either. Henry wasn't interested in food.

When the dog lay down on command she said: *At last something that Henry can do!*

Henry didn't bother going back.

Not only is that rude, sarcastic and insulting to both Henry and his owner but displays a lack of understanding of dog behaviour and a range of sound training techniques.

Can't you stop your dog barking?

No, that's why I came here for help as you are a dog trainer.

Well take it outside until it calms down and then bring it in again. And so she did. Again. And again. And again.

Translation: I don't know how to stop a dog barking.

Can't you stop your dog barking? Part Two.

No, that's why I came here for training.

Well go to the end of the hall. The trainer then surrounded the dog and owner with chairs and then put blankets over the chairs so the dog could not see the other dogs (but obviously it could still hear them, dumbass!) Guess what – it did not work.

I know what I am doing.

At one class the trainer had the habit of going to every dog and giving it a treat. One owner asked him politely not to feed his dog. "I know what I'm doing" snapped the trainer as he fed the dog a treat.

What he was doing was inadvertently training a dog to accept food from strangers and make it think it perfectly acceptable to sniff complete strangers' hands, a very dangerous habit as someone who does not like dogs could accuse your dog of trying to bite them and that could lead to all sorts of trouble.

I would NEVER feed someone else's dog or allow my dog to be fed by someone else.

How do you know it isn't poisoned or such cheap rubbish it may give your dog diarrhoea?

Once a dog has bitten a human it's best to have it put down.

Translation: I don't know how to fix this and this dog is scary so kill it.

Obviously I am very biased as Jack my Cocker Spaniel was about to be put down for biting a human and he was quite vicious. Now people cannot believe that he was a biter as he trots up to them, tail wagging and loving a bit of fuss.

Possessive poodle

Benji the miniature poodle was possessive over such things as toys, socks and gloves. He growled at and nipped his owners but responded well to the new methods.

URBAN MYTH

YOU SHOULD IGNORE YOUR DOGS WHEN YOU COME HOME.

WRONG!

I don't know where this idea came from but I can see why somebody suggested it.

A person goes to work. The dogs are left alone for a few hours. The person comes home from work.

The dogs are extremely happy to see the owner and get excited, barking, jumping up running around etc.

The owner is also happy to see the dogs and feels wanted, excited and usually a bit guilty for leaving the dogs alone. The owner greets the dogs enthusiastically and this eventually leads to the dogs greeting EVERYONE in the same way.

So some bright spark decided that to keep the dogs calmer it would be best to ignore the dogs for five minutes before saying hello and it entered into the folklore of 'REALLY CRAP DOG TRAINING Volume 1'.

I advise my clients to adopt a much more natural way of greeting your dogs.

On occasion I have taken one of my dogs to the vets, and left the others at home. When we returned I noticed the other dogs would ignore me at first and go nose to nose with the other dog and then sniff all around them before coming to me.

It seemed that they were saying "Where have you been? Who have you been with? Have you had any food and have you brought anything for us?"

(Very similar to a wife and kids really! I know that's politically incorrect but it makes me smile and it's my book after all.)

The whole process took about 20 seconds and then they all carried on as normal. Nobody ignored anyone else. We all said hello quietly and moved on.

So I started to adapt the same behaviour when I got home. I would stop and say hello quite calmly for 10 or 20 seconds and then move on into the house. It seemed much more natural than ignoring the dogs I wanted to greet, I just didn't go overboard in my excitement. I kept calm and copied my dogs.

CHAPTER 23

Nervous dogs

I have worked with many dogs that show signs of nervousness.

In my experience there appear to be several different reasons why these dogs have this problem.

Firstly, it can be traced back to the litter, although I have only come across a few dogs like this.

I visited a Standard Poodle called Lady Gaga and she had been the puppy nervously watching from the back of the litter when people were selecting their new puppies. She is now five years old and a complete basket case because she has been unsure of humans and other dogs all her life. However she is a smart dog and we soon calmed her down. She stopped turning into a whirling dervish when visitors arrived at the house by teaching her owners to control the space.

Secondly, the dog can become nervous after being attacked by another dog when young. If they don't feel supported and protected by their owner they can either become very timid and not want to go for walks at all or they become nervous aggressive. When I say nervous aggressive I mean the dog will be on constant alert when on the lead and will bark, lunge and generally make a huge fuss to avoid contact with another dog.

Their owner cannot control the dog and ends up avoiding other dogs. The dog then becomes isolated and never gets to have a calm walk or mix with other dogs.

Lastly, the nervousness stems from abuse from a human. I find this very common in dogs that have been used for breeding in puppy farms and then discarded when their usefulness is over.

It is also quite common with rescue dogs where people have taken on a puppy and the dog has not been trained properly. The puppy jumps up, mouths and nips the owners in puppy play and chews the house to pieces. The human's anger and frustration at the dog's bad behaviour ends up with the dog being punished and abused and the dog learns to fear humans. It will try to show submission by cowering and retreating to a corner but will growl and snarl if approached because it feels the need to defend itself.

Some of dogs I see have been taken to puppy classes but according to reports, the standard of training is very poor. The puppy classes appear to be taught by the most inexperienced trainers because the senior trainers are only interested in teaching the advanced obedience classes.

One client of mine was asked to leave a puppy class after two sessions and later found out that out of ten puppies only two stayed to the end of the course. However, there were no refunds given.

Soothing and reassurance

Dog owners face a huge problem when deciding which dog training route to take. Many clients contact me because they have been confused by conflicting advice, their dog is confused because it has been subjected to many different techniques and methods which haven't worked and they need something that both dog and owner can understand quickly.

Soothing and reassurance to a troubled dog is counter-productive.

If you try and soothe and reassure a dog by stroking and using a nice voice you are using the same signals as when you praise a dog, wouldn't you agree?

So if that dog is nervous, unbalanced and fearful you are saying to the dog **"Hey, it's okay to be like that"** because you are using praise signals. You are not going to make the dog any better; you are going to make the dog worse **because you are reinforcing the behaviour**.

The dog needs leadership, direction and correction and it will become calm and balanced. You don't have to be cruel or unkind to achieve this.

With nervous dogs I usually get the owner to put them on a lead and then take the lead and make the dog stay within a couple of feet of me. Then I **appear** to do nothing. I ignore the dog and chat to the owners so that the dog realises that I have seen its submissive signals and understand it is no threat to me. By ignoring it I am showing it that I am no threat either. I will then take the dog for a walk and then, with the owner holding his dog, I will bring out my dogs and fuss them so that the nervous dog can see how my dogs trust me and enjoy my attention. If the dog's body language is good I will allow it to meet my dogs and we normally go for a pack walk together. The nervous dog will pick up the calm pack behaviour and start to relax and to trust me. It is amazing the difference one can make in only a couple of hours.

How many times do you see a dog owner saying "be nice, be nice" as their dog lunges towards another dog?

What they should be saying is "don't you dare get us into a pack fight. Stay calm, ignore them and follow my lead".

The dog needs correction – not affection.

IN SUMMARY...
IF YOUR DOG DOES NOT UNDERSTAND YOU...

WHO'S TO BLAME? YOU OR THE DOG?

A dog does not do things to annoy you.

Dogs love a strong leader because they prefer to follow.

I've never seen a dog treat another dog.

I've never seen a dog praise another dog.

Treat or clicker training is not the answer to everything.

Get the right balance between discipline and affection.

I love my dogs but I make sure I remind them who is in charge every day.

And finally...

If you use the General and Sentry method correctly it is an immensely powerful tool to control your dog anywhere.

BLOCK
BARGE
BARK
PARENT STARE

BUSTER

9TH OCTOBER 2004 –
9TH NOVEMBER 2015

King of the Terriers,
a gentle giant among dogs.

This book is dedicated to the many dog owners
who refused to give up hope with their dogs,
even when their dog had destroyed their home
or bitten another dog or human being.

Their faith in me has been uplifting, and their
gratitude humbling.

I love dogs, and my aim is to give people
a natural way to train their dogs, an alternative
to treat training.

THE RESULTS SPEAK
FOR THEMSELVES.